Ireland

A WEEK IN THE LIFE OF A NATION

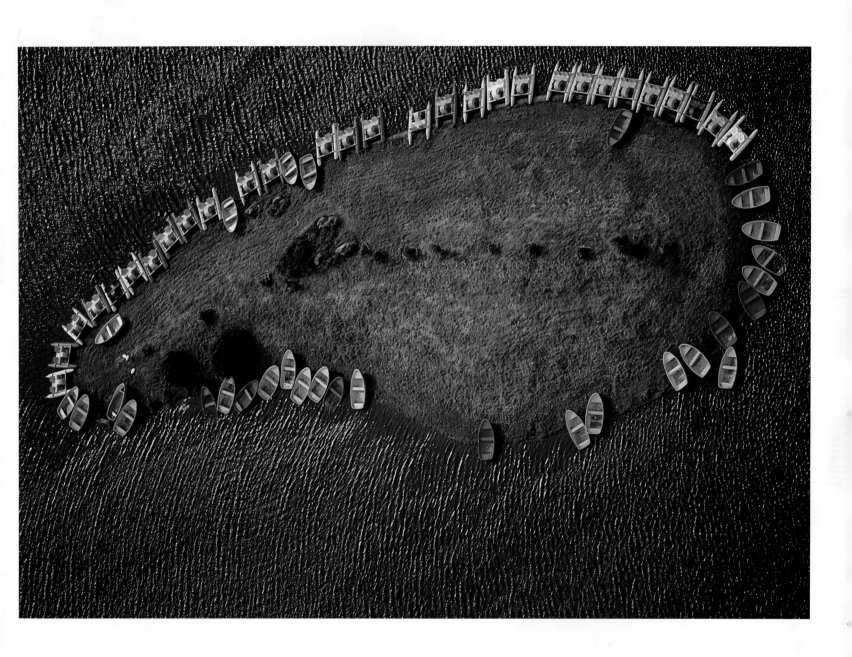

Ireland

A WEEK IN THE LIFE OF A NATION

EDITED BY RED SAUNDERS & SYD SHELTON • TEXT BY ANTHONY CRONIN

CENTURY PUBLISHING

LONDON

First published in 1986 by Century Hutchinson Ltd,
Brookmount House, 62-65 Chandos Place, Covent Garden, London WC2N 4NW

Set in Helvetica by Stratatype, London

Printed by The Pot Still Press Pty Ltd, Sydney, Australia

British Library Cataloguing in Publication Data

Ireland: a week in the life of a nation.
1. Ireland—Description and travel—1981—Views
I. Saunders, Red   II. Shelton, Syd
941.50824'022'2   DA982

ISBN 0-7126-9518-4

EDITORS	**Red Saunders, Syd Shelton**
MANAGING EDITOR	**John Ellis**
ADMINISTRATOR	**Kim Armitage**
TEXT	**Anthony Cronin**
CONSULTANT EDITOR	**Brian Trench**
CAPTIONS	**Fintan O'Toole, Andy Pollak, Brian Trench**
RESEARCH EDITORS	**Jerry Fitzpatrick, Grainne Morby**
RESEARCH	**Jude Bowles, Bill Hayes**
EDITORIAL CONSULTANTS	**Sister Benvenuta, Michael Cunningham, Luke Gibbons, Paul Gillespie, David Hammond, Mary Holland, Nuala Ó Faoláin, Breandán Ó hEithir, Dermot O'Shea, Andy Pollak, Derek Speirs**
DESIGN AND ART EDITOR	**Syd Shelton**
ASSISTANT TO THE ART EDITOR	**Red Saunders**
DESIGN AND ART PRODUCTION	**Phil Levene**
PICTURE EDITORS	**Bruce Bernard (London), Ellen Madere (New York)**
DUBLIN OFFICE	**Claire Byrne, Eddie Conlon, Jennifer O'Neill**
LONDON OFFICE	**Maggy Moody**
PRODUCTION ASSISTANT	**Julian J**
E6 COLOUR PROCESSING	**Ceta (London), PCL (Dublin), L&I (New York)**
BLACK & WHITE PRINTING	**Adrian Ensor (London)**
OFFICIAL PHOTOGRAPHIC CONSULTANT	**Kodak Ireland Limited**
PHOTOGRAPHIC MATERIALS	**Kodak Ireland Limited, Polaroid (UK) Limited**
HOTELS	**Jurys Hotel Group**
COMPUTERS	**Orbact Total Computing, Dublin**

Contents

Editors' Notes

Ireland: A Week in the Life of a Nation started over a late brunch in a 24-hour kosher deli in Los Angeles where Red Saunders, Syd Shelton and John Ellis were slumped after an exhausting day's shoot for the 1984 photo-project, **24 Hours in the Life of Los Angeles.** Mark Garner, the Australian printer of **A Day in the Life of London,** had been invited to join them to study at first hand the hectic mechanics of constructing the project with a view to financing an even more adventurous project: Ireland In One Week. He liked what he had seen, he liked the London book, he liked the odds on Ireland – and left for the airport with the classic entrepreneurial line, "Get some figures to me and we'll see if we can work out a deal." That was how it began.

The whole idea for these projects goes back to **Life** magazine's **Day in the Life of the USA** which had been the inspiration for the photo-book format; but research reveals that Rodchenko, the Soviet constructivist artist, in the 1920s mounted an extraordinary event that he called **A Day in the Life of the**

World when he invited artists from all over the planet to submit every conceivable type of "art", from ceramics to photographs. Red Saunders as a photographer and Syd Shelton as a designer were both invited to work on **A Day in the Life of New Zealand** and it was while on location there that the limitations of attempting to photograph a country in a day became apparent. So, excited by the concept, they decided to photograph a whole city in a day rather than a whole country, hence the two projects **A Day in the Life of London** and **24 Hours in the Life of Los Angeles.** For this new project they decided on a week including the weekend.

It had been their intention to make a book about Ireland before the **24 Hours in the Life of Los Angeles** project arose. Once the Ireland project was accepted and backed by Mark Garner and they were travelling around setting it up in Ireland – whether in a hotel in Killibegs, a bed and breakfast boarding house in Kiltimagh or on the **Pat Kenny Show** on Radio Telefis Eireann – the question always came up: why Ireland? Why should image-makers from London want to make a photo-book about Ireland?

Well, above all else, Ireland is the perfect candidate for having its picture taken. It is probably one of the most beautiful countries in Northern Europe. Physically and practically, you can drive from one side to the other in a day, and of course they speak the same language.

Secondly, it is a deeply religious country, partitioned and still in political conflict; it is a country hesitating at the rural and urban crossroads. They felt that in some way, however small, they could tell a real story in a week of Ireland's life that would challenge the banality of the general British prejudice against the Irish.

Most serious observers would agree that "photography" is in poor shape at the moment; indeed many would say it is an endangered species.

If you look on the bookshelves you will find many photo-books on Ireland. Why then is this one different? Most photo-books are photo library books – that's to say, a collection of images from different photographers and different photo libraries over varying periods of time, or they are the work of one or two individual photographers taken over a long period. This book is like a time capsule; the Ireland you see here is the one they found in that last week of August 1985, and they hope that it will redress the balance.

With preliminary wheeling and dealing out of the way, they signed the contract in January 1985. First they prepared a brochure to get some sponsorship in Ireland because the figures they worked out for the backers made the project certainly too expensive. So, brochure in hand, John Ellis and Red Saunders played fund-raisers through the autumn and winter of 1984/85, lugging a video presentation kit around a maze of boardrooms, executive offfices and hotel rooms. Many prospective backers turned them down once they realised they weren't doing a bland Bord Fáilte (Irish Tourist Board) promotion and that they were including coverage of the North. "The North?" they would ask with a worried look in their eyes. Trying to make a book with some kind of serious photographic statement does not lend itself to corporate and governmental sponsorship. The main candidates for sponsorship soon became clear — hotel, film, and computing groups.

Back in London they started to select photographers for the project from the USA, UK and Europe. The Irish photographers they would go and see in the early summer. When recruiting they asked them what was their passion, their excitement about the project and they tried to mix that with the editorial requirements. They invited an extraordinary array of photographers, from those with worldwide fame to unknown young talent. Documentary photographers gave up their bread & butter assignments to focus their subjective lenses on the social issues seldom seen outside Ireland. The highly-skilled advertising photographers were prised from their £1000 a day studios and relocated to the windswept passes of Donegal. No fees were paid, they provided travel, accommodation, film, Polaroid and basic expenses — the deal was the same for all.

Brian Trench was the main organizer in Dublin and had put together an impressive Editorial Consultant team for a brainstorm session. They booked a small conference room and lunch and talked all day with 12 people (all listed under consultants in the front of this book). They discussed over innumerable cups of coffee the purpose in doing this book; all had different ideas but all were agreed that the portrayal of Ireland by most photographic books was clichéd and seeking to return to a past era. They also came up with a long list of possible subjects. These suggestions together with the general pointers went into a series of briefing documents sent to international photographers as they were signed up.

They now had the basis of the Dublin team and a network for hundreds of contacts all over Ireland. They had to piece the puzzle together and work out the system, a cross reference for the great filing cabinet of life. To bring photographers from the US and Europe, find the guides and assistants, hotel accommodation, car hire, air tickets and connecting flights, customs problems, equipment hire, to organise a dozen different film requirements, b&w, colour, in various formats, translators and insurance seemed the straightforward part of the operation.

Pre-production intensified through May, June and July, then the whole London-based operation loaded into vans and moved lock, stock and tripod to Dublin where they joined the Irish team. The admin team had done its job well. A big, old house had been rented in Dún Laoghaire where the whole London team stayed.

Production offices were rented in Dame Street, central Dublin where a communication system was already in existence with telex facilities, 26 phone lines and a mailing address.

Sponsored computers moved in; Londoners met Dubliners. They had portfolios to view, brainstorms about what to shoot, editorial considerations to decide on, and the need to log and assimilate an enormous amount of information. They had huge countdown charts in the offices and soon every wall was covered with every conceivable type of information. The phones rang daytime, evening and night. Every room felt crammed with staff as the first day of the shoot got closer and nearer and a subtle, collective hysteria covered everyone. While this organization was in progress, they had to create in media terms what is known as the big M, MOMENTUM. So in the middle of all the daily madness that the office was fast becoming, they had TV crews setting up lights, and reporters pushing microphones into their faces with questions ranging from "Do you believe photography can change people's lives?" to "Why Ireland?".

As the production office was set-up, they drove off in a 14-year-old VW campervan on a 2500-mile round-Ireland trip, to visit places they had never been before, check locations discussed in sessions and meet the potential guides and assistants recruited earlier by Brian Trench. The trip was exhausting but invaluable. The light, so special to photographers, was quite extraordinary: the four seasons every day. The atmosphere, the moods and the images from tiny villages in Mayo to army checkpoints in Crossmaglen lodged themselves in their minds. They returned to base with cardboard boxes full of location information and contacts to start the massive task of creating a county by county, photographer by photographer, cross reference bible. From then on it was fine-tuning all the way and hour upon hour of debating among themselves what to select from these hundreds of locations. After all, they were making one book in five days, not a 10-part encyclopaedia set on Ireland.

They had set up a portable studio in the Campaign HQ at Jury's Hotel. Bellhops shoved panic-packed mesages under the door and the phones were engaged 18 hours a day. TV interviews were held in one room, radio in another.

Assistants snored on sofas as they held yet another 2.00am crisis meeting, energy sustained by continuous room service, Bushmills, ice and sandwiches. Last minute dramas appeared and disappeared: photographers missed ferries, others were found drunk and disorderly, one American had to be replaced by another photographer at 4.00 in the morning, and all this while the photographers – impatient to rush off to their locations – had to be kept herded into one place in order to participate in the publicity. One photographer had even been hit by a rubber bullet the week before in Derry and was involved with two others in a car crash on the night before the shoot started (though happily not seriously hurt). One or two photographers had been given the Editors' permission to shoot a couple of days outside the shoot period due to personal reasons.

The week of the shoot, when it finally arrived, seemed to pass very quickly. The Americans arrived a few days early to recover from travel lag. Europeans next, then finally, locals. They had briefings in groups of about ten. Photographers received their survival packs with details of the assignment. They left the meeting with carrier bags splitting with film, Polaroids, t-shirts, umbrellas. They had their photos taken twice, once for their Project I-D tags and once for the back of the book. The rehearsal was over. The deadline was now.

That was when the rain began to trickle down the photographers' anoraks. On every day of August it rained, somewhere in Ireland. And rained. It was to be the wettest August ever recorded at most weather observation stations.

The phones at the Dublin office were oddly silent that week. Had the photographers all been washed away? But maybe this was a good sign; at least there were no distress calls. As the photographers trooped back to the base at Jury's Hotel, it became clear that the weather had become a creative challenge. When the rain had suddenly stopped the moments of sunshine were all the more dramatic. And for every rendezvous missed, there was the eventful chance encounter.

For this project it was decided that they wanted more words, but not just purple adjectives, so they approached the Irish writer and poet Anthony Cronin to collaborate with them.

Returning to London, turning the tiny Soho offices into a design studio, installing a PMT camera and all the layout equipment. They were joined by Phil Levene for art and production, Bruce Bernard, one of London's most respected picture editors, and Ellen Madere, a startlingly fresh eye from New York, for the huge task of editing 200,000 images down to approximately 250. Three weeks saw it accomplished. While spreads started to be designed, copies were sent back and forth to caption-writers in Dublin. Endless debate raged about the front cover. The deadline crawled closer, the night-shift panic took over, and, with the wax still wet on the artwork, Syd Shelton boarded the plane for the printers in Australia.

This book is not a comprehensive view of Ireland, that is not what they set out to achieve. The team could shoot for three months and never accomplish that. What you see here is a combination of the direction in which they pointed them, their own visual spontaneity with their own editorial style. The photographs are not illustrations, they are the whole point — they are the book.

Rural Dreams and Urban Wakings

Towns in Ireland are a fairly recent invention. Of what may be reckoned the principal centres of habitation, less than a third were in existence before 1600, a time when most European cities were already ancient.

They are also a foreign import. The Gaelic Irish positively disliked urban living; and although a case has been made for the suggestion that the early Christian monasteries were urban complexes of a sort, the first true townships were built by the Norsemen as late as the 10th century.

When, somewhat later, Dublin became the centre of English rule in Ireland, the natives entered it with fear and wonder and departed from it for the green and unpolluted spaces of the countryside with relief. Of course, they were also unwelcome. For centuries various forms of apartheid were the settlers' defence against inundation. Dublin, like most places of consequence, still has an "Irishtown", but these shanty settlements usually huddled outside the walls.

And some of the native distrust of the town still remains. In Ireland, as elsewhere, the 19th century saw a huge exodus from the countryside. But for a very long time it was to the cities of other countries, to New York and Boston, Liverpool and Birmingham, that the Irish went.

They eventually learned, in America at least, to use the city, to become, even, adepts of its dark wisdoms, but their songs and their stories, their legends and their loyalties, still celebrated and related to a rural past.

To a marked extent they still do. Since the early 1960s Dublin has been the principal beneficiary of the Irish participation in the worldwide desertion of the country for the town. But it has become in some ways an ad hoc place, many of whose inhabitants do not feel quite at home or quite at ease there. This is partly perhaps because the degree of commitment to it in establishment circles has always been low. There has been a rural bias in most Irish art and literature for the past 60 years or so, an assumption that somehow the rural reality was more real and intense as well as being more colourful and picturesque than the urban. For many years after the institution of a state broadcasting service it was staffed by people to whom the words culture, Irish and rural were apparently inseparable. Even if there was such a thing as a Dublin culture, it was not Gaelic or even native. And in any case Dublin had, in spite of Robert Emmet, the United Irishmen and the Citizen Army, a bad national record. It was West British, Protestant and snobbish in outlook. It had been on friendly terms with its large British garrison. It had jeered the rebels as they were marched out of the GPO in 1916.

Certainly nothing was done to dignify it as a capital. With the exception of the Ministry of Commerce in Kildare Street and the Bus Station, which is awkwardly situated behind the Custom House, the state has failed to commission any new buildings, preferring to house its bureaucracy in the havens provided by the old British regime or by private enterprise. When the era of speculative development came to Dublin in the 1960s the authorities presided in seeming helplessness over the destruction of much fine Georgian architecture and its replacement by fifth-rate office buildings. And though the inner-city slums were cleared eventually, the grey new working-class housing estates and the middle-class suburbs spread blindly westward or climbed into the foothills of the Dublin mountains as if searching for some lost rural arcadia which had been left behind.

And the psychology of many of the newer inhabitants of Dublin would suggest that it was. Every Friday night the buses for Roscommon and Rathcormack, Clonmel and Kilmallock are packed with girls who work in city offices during the week, who indeed sleep, cook and wash in the thin-walled apartments into which the old red-brick houses of south Dublin have been converted, but who do not choose to regard themselves as more than temporary residents of the capital. And even those higher up the jobs ladder, the males who have attained to pensionable posts or professional status in the city, and who rear their families there, sometimes exhibit what seems an unnatural degree of nostalgia for their parish of origin.

Whether this truly encompasses a yearning for the primitive is doubtful, whatever the prestige of the primitive myth in literature and elsewhere. The hinterland from which they have come has, in its turn, been transformed in recent years. State grants for houses in rural areas have meant the end of the dilapidated farmhouse with its often weed-grown roof; and if the architectural results are sometimes odd, it is because they come from pattern-books that include miniature versions of what might be southern California style haciendas. Rural electrification, one of the catch-cries of the forties and fifties, is now an accomplished fact, which has meant not only the end of the oil-lamp but the advent of the television, blinking through every living-room window in the land. And outside almost every door there is the motor car, with its ever-insistent suggestion that there is some place more exciting to go than just to a neighbour's house for a game of cards.

Much of this increase in comfort and consumerism is due not only to state and EEC packages and subsidies for farmers, but to a perhaps more durable prosperity based on a reduction of numbers. Those who remain are the beneficiaries of a long process of clearance which began with the Encumbered Estates Act of 1849. It was of course the weakest economically, the labourers, the cottiers and the smallest holders who were cleared, who took their places on the emigrant boats with younger sons and unmarried daughters, a tide not stemmed until the 1960s. In almost any other country — certainly in any of the developing industrial economies of Europe — such an exodus would have ended in the cities of the same state, though there would have been some emigration to America as well. But in southern Ireland there was virtually no industry or anything else to absorb such a multitude, and so they vanished, an almost dumb mass, voiceless in the land from which they had been uprooted.

The result has been an unnatural lopsidedness, in politics, culture and everything else. Although towards the end of the 1960s the number of dwellers in urban areas began to be more than those in rural, the pattern of Irish politics and much else had been set: two large parties with a bias towards the agricultural proprietors and their values, a weak Labour party which did not even command the loyalty of the industrial proletariat, let alone those who swelled the ranks of the civil service and the new bureaucracies of finance and insurance.

Since that brief era of job creation is now over, we may expect new patterns in the future. The population of the Republic has grown dramatically in recent years; and it is now increasingly young, urban and unemployed, with more than a third of the total in greater Dublin. Both culturally and politically it may for some time be a question of new wine in old bottles, but if it remains so too long, the bottles are likely to burst.

Modernity and tradition combined are typical of the west coast town of Galway. Across the fast-flowing river Corrib is Claddagh Quay, once a separate Irish-speaking fishing village from which the city itself developed as a fishing and trading centre. Galway has long been unusually cosmopolitan, with strong Spanish and Anglo-Norman influences intertwining with the native Gaelic culture. More recent influences in the shape of multi-national industry such as the giant Digital Equipment Corporation, the influx of refugees from the rat race, and the presence of a university have helped shield Galway from the worst of the economic depression and have contributed to a burgeoning cultural life.

Days before this picture was taken, the harbour area was assaulted by firework-throwing Catalan actors as part of the Galway Arts Festival. The nearby Druid Theatre celebrated ten years of existence during which the company has gone from isolated provincial status to being Ireland's alternative national theatre. And between 23rd August and 25th August, buskers from several countries took part in an International Busking Festival.

Following pages:

Deep-water berthing facilities, a suitable construction site, ample water, energy and labour supplies, tax incentives and capital support (£16.8 million) from the state were among the inducements for a consortium of three of the world's leading metal companies to build a £600 million alumina reducer at Aughinish (centre background) on the estuary of the river Shannon. Over 1½ million tonnes of bauxite are brought each year from Guinea and 800,000 tonnes of alumina are shipped out to smelters in continental Europe where aluminium is produced.

The world's largest aluminium producer, the Canadian-owned Alcan corporation, became the controlling shareholder of the County Limerick factory in 1985 when it bought out the stake of its former partner, Anaconda. And just two years after production commenced in September 1983, Alcan was reported to be considering closing the Irish plant because of the international over-supply of alumina. Pressure mounted on the Irish government to give additional aid in the form of low-price natural gas from the offshore field off County Cork.

The port town of Foynes (foreground) was the base for the first transatlantic flights – by seaplane – to and from Ireland. These began in 1937 and continued until Shannon Airport was opened in 1945 directly across the estuary on the northern side.

JOEL STERNFELD

MARTIN PARR

During the 1960s much of the Georgian centre of Dublin was given over to office and commercial development and the centres of housing development were shifted out to the suburbs. For the poor, the destination was the Ballymun high-rise flats complex on the unfashionable northside, the country's only major high-rise housing development.

Preceding pages:

For those who were moving up in the world, the southside suburbs beckoned.
Ballymun still has the highest concentration of poverty in the country and much of its population is a shifting one, with families moving in to the flats while they wait for a house elsewhere. Those who have stayed have tried to build a community and to give a personal touch to the flats with the help of the itinerant carpet dealers. While in 1985 the great housing boom of the early eighties was in something of a decline, the southside suburbs, unlike the vast estates of houses to the west, remained fashionable. Ireland still has an extraordinarily high rate of home ownership and the desire to own your own house has remained as one of the constants of Irish life, encouraged by the low rate of local authority building.

MARTIN PARR

their small home with Swanies the
swans, Flossie the fox, Rosie the dog,
Pussy Cat, and a silver pheasant, with
all of whom they keep up unceasing
conversation. Now in their 70s, the
Hall brothers have lived all their lives
here in Owenstown, near Killinick,
where their parents and grand-
parents also lived.

Preceding pages:

It is 7.45 a.m. on 23rd August. The
hay has to be saved. But first Paddy
and Jer Minihane have breakfast —
served up to them by Ina Minihane,
Paddy's wife. The two brothers farm
50 acres at Drishanemore, near
Skibbereen, County Cork, keeping a
herd of 15 dairy cows, and fishing in
the sea lapping against their farm
when the land does not keep them
busy.

JOHN LONDEI

An IRA firing party pays perpetual and silent tribute to the organisation's dead on a Derry gable end. This mural commemorates the death of two IRA activists shot in December 1984 by under-cover British soldiers in the grounds of a Derry hospital. They were armed and it would seem that they were about to launch some action; but they were shot without challenge or interrogation. The republican murals of Belfast and Derry perpetuate the memory of the IRA's members who have died in action or on hunger strike. They mingle the religious, the revolutionary and the rhetorical in a unique combination. The political messages are sometimes supported by distinctly Catholic imagery of suffering and sacrifice.

BARRIE ROKEACH

The tailor's business is no longer. Patrick O'Grady has passed on. But the neat shop front, the unusual moulded door and the striking sign-writing which declared his presence and his premises in Quay Road, Westport, County Mayo, are carefully conserved. In summer 1985, a youth employment scheme refurbished the door, sign and façade. And in summer 1985, some of Patrick O'Grady's 12 scattered children returned to the family home from their present homes in Britain and the United States. The house is only occasionally used for such visits.

Lil Horkan (centre) was going shopping, Kitty Nelis (right) was working in her house and Mona Navin (extreme left) was in her dressing gown having a cup of tea when, as she recalls, "the photographer kept saying 'come on, come on'," and she joined neighbour Barbara Greezy on the doorstep.

Westport is a tidy town, an occasional winner of the hotly contested National Tidy Towns competition. Westport was re-built to a planned lay-out in the 1770s so that the streets related to the sloping site.

Preceding pages:

"Rakes" of wagons run slowly on a special bog railway of temporary tracks hauling in the peat from Derrygreenagh Bog, County Offaly, for compressing into briquettes and fuelling a power station.

The peat is scraped from the top layer of the bog by a machine which stretches 30 metres across the bog and inches along as it lifts the peat and passes it to the wagons for transport to this marshalling yard (left). From there it goes either to the Croghan briquette factory or the Ferbane power station.

In the few breaks in the weather, agricultural contractors worked frantically with their combine harvesters (right), having more breakdowns and getting stuck more often than usual because of the difficult conditions.

Sunday 25th August was a rare reward for Irish holidaymakers who had stayed at home; on the east coast there were sunny spells amid the showers. Courtown, a beach on the County Wexford coast, is traditionally popular with working-class Dublin people, easily accessible by train and providing a long clear beach of white sand.

Before foreign package holidays came within reach of working-class pockets, beaches like Bettystown to the north of Dublin (evoked by the writer Neil Jordan in his story **Night in Tunisia**) and Courtown to the south, provided the main holiday destinations for Dubliners.

Depending largely on visitors of modest means, Courtown is an unpretentious resort, providing accommodation in caravans, chalets, cottages and even tents. But it does also have candy floss, slot machines, dodgems and chips.

MARTIN PARR

When the high tide of hippie hopes
ebbed away, a faithful few were left
beached on the west coast of Ireland.
Geoff Pearson's house at the Dawn of
Hope Bridge, Greagh-na-Glaogh,
Drumkerrin, County Leitrim, is a rare
outpost of the dream of getting back
to the garden.

Leitrim is the poorest and most
sparsely populated county in Ireland,
and much of the land is wet, hilly and
infertile. Its high levels of emigration
and declining population mean that
land is available relatively cheaply, even
to foreigners. But the challenge of
surviving on a self-sufficient small
holding is at its greatest here. The
Pearsons, seen here with friends and
neighbours, the Bowes, the Brosnans,
the Sweeneys and Dettlef Wedde run
such a smallholding. The dried flowers
above the mantelpiece are one of their
products.

The village of Doolin in County Clare
(below) attracts more transient visitors
in the summer, but the quest for
sparsely populated countryside and
traditional lifestyles is the same. In the
summer, the pub music sessions are
packed with the visitors, some of
whom are themselves exponents of
traditional Irish music.

The county has a vigorous musical
tradition. At the Willie Clancy school in
Milltown Malbay, earlier in the month, a
notable County Clare piper was
remembered and his legacy relived in
piping workshops and sessions. At the
Merriman summer school in
Lisdoonvarna, on the same weekend
as this picture was taken, one of the
big successes, amid the discussion of
problems of society and state, was the
organisation of Clare set dancing
lessons in the town square.

MIKE ABRAHAMS △ DAVID HURN ▷

Few cities in Britain or Ireland have such a magnificent setting as Belfast. It stands at the head of a deep sea lough between the spectacular basalt cliffs and heather-covered slopes of Cave Hill and Black Mountain and the green fields of the Castlereagh Hills.

Within and around the city itself every view is dominated by the huge gantries of the Harland and Wolff shipyard, "Goliath" and "Samson".

The shipyard was founded in 1851 and was taken over by a Yorkshire engineer, Edward Harland, in 1858. Harland and Wolff's workforce, 9,000 strong at the turn of the century, had risen by the early 1950s to a peak of 21,000, all but a few hundred of them Protestant, and the yard had become a symbol of Protestant prosperity and pride at being part of the United Kingdom.

But the shipyard in common with shipyards in Britain and elsewhere, has declined over the past 20 years. Harland and Wolff was taken over by the British government. In 1985, it employed barely 5,000 people and required a huge subsidy to cover its £36 million losses.

Following pages:

Major Graeme Cooper and the 1st Battalion, The Green Howards, under his command, were in enemy territory in the Lower Falls Road area, the most deprived and the most pro-IRA in Belfast.

The huge cotton and linen mills that used to dominate and provide employment in the area are long since closed, empty hulks which local people are trying, with some government assistance, to turn into workshops and community centres. Unemployment in parts of the Lower Falls – such as the Divis Flats complex, one of Europe's most notorious modern high rise slums – is over 80%. The Lower Falls was also the first area in Belfast to be affected by the violence of the "Troubles", when Catholics were attacked by the police and Protestant mobs in summer 1969, three people were killed, scores of houses were burned and hundreds of families forced to flee their homes.

In the following year, the area was cordoned off by the British Army for two days while it searched for arms, and five people died in the ensuing battles with Republicans.

During the 1981 republican hunger strike the Lower Falls was the scene of nightly demonstrations, street protests and riots, and two people died and dozens were injured as the police fired plastic bullets to break up crowds.

CHARLES TRAUB

COWARDLY
LOYALISTS
BACK UT

At Enniscrone, County Sligo, seasonal visitors and some regular local customers keep arthritis, rheumatism and hang-overs at bay with hot seaweed baths. They were built at the small, traditional resort in 1912 by the father of the present owner, Edward Kilcullen, seen in the picture. He and his wife, Maura, intend to keep Kilcullen's Hot Sea Water Baths going, although a farm is their main business. Indeed, Mrs Kilcullen immerses herself in the iodine-rich weed and salty water every day. Business at the baths was poor in August 1985, about one third of the usual custom at that time of the year, the Killcullens reckoned. But bathers arrived on this day in a steady flow — and left with a healthy glow.

The only other seaweed baths in Ireland are at Ballybunion, County Kerry. At the height of the normally busy August holiday season, there were few takers for such rigorous pleasures; the sky was leaden, the sea was angry and the beach was deserted.

The seaweed, which the Atlantic sweeps in plentifully, also provides fertiliser for coastal farmers and is gathered by hundreds of part-time collectors for export to Scotland. After processing, it goes further afield for use in a range of several hundred different products.

Preceding pages:

Belfast's "black taxis" have become a familiar sight on the Catholic Falls Road, as seen here, and on the Protestant Shankill Road over the past 13 years. They run on fixed routes, carry up to eight passengers and are cheaper, quicker and more frequent than the city's bus service.

They first appeared on the streets in 1972, when riots and shoot-outs between the IRA and the British Army kept most of the buses out of working class areas of Catholic West Belfast. Sonny O'Reilly went to London and bought five six-year-old London taxis for £190. There are now over 400 of them in West and North Belfast, and despite frequent threats by the British government's licensing and transport authorities to force them off the road, they are still the most popular form of transport for thousands of people in the city's most deprived areas.

They also give employment to nearly 900 men, many of them former prisoners. In Catholic areas, the drivers pay a weekly subscription to the IRA's prisoners' welfare fund, and in Protestant areas they are also believed to contribute to paramilitary funds.

DENIS WAUGH

Housing estates built in the 1970s have changed dramatically the character of Greystones, a County Wicklow town 20 miles south of Dublin. The prim little harbour town whose higher-than-average Protestant, and elderly, population gave it a distinctive identity, has become a commuter town with a young population in search of work. The announcement in June 1985 that US micro-electronics manufacturers, Advanced Micro Devices (AMD) were to establish their European plant here seemed to mark the most dramatic change in the character of a town with no major source of employment.

But in November, AMD let it be known that they had postponed their Irish investment plan – possibly for years. Most of the working population would continue to leave Greystones in the mornings and return in the evenings.

The demand was raised for the electric-powered commuter train service, commissioned in 1984, to be extended the five miles from Bray to Greystones.

Greystones has a couple of hotels which have long lost any tourist function, catering now for social functions of professional bodies, a sailing club, a golf club and a rugby club and it still retains a proportion of Protestants over twice the 3½% average for the Republic.

Following pages

The cliffs of Moher (right) have long been a mandatory port of call on every round Ireland tour. The tower was erected here in 1835 by Sir Cornelius O'Brien, Member of Parliament, for "strangers visiting the magnificent scenery of this neighbourhood". Today strangers drive into a large car park, alive with mobile burger-vans, ice-cream vendors, tourist donkey carts, leprechaun stickers and hot chips.

In the crevices between the rocks of the Burren (left) a varied and exotic flora thrives. On the bare limestone hills, there are herds of wild goats. Below is a largely unexplored labyrinth of caves and passages. And in the valleys and villages, refugees from the cities of Ireland, Britain and continental Europe seek a simpler life-style.

BARRIE ROKEACH

FRANK MILLER

The poet William Butler Yeats, who is buried in Drumcliffe churchyard, County Sligo, on the far side of Ben Bulben – the looming table mountain in the background – dreamt of an ideal peasantry "cold and passionate as the dawn". Though born in Dublin, he used the landscape around Ben Bulben as the territory of Celtic Twilight romanticism.

Over the two weeks before this picture was taken, international academics and visiting students were dissecting his achievement at the annual Yeats International Summer School held in Sligo town.

The students, the joggers, and a juke box that stands in front of a garish mural of Yeats in the Drumcliffe pub, opposite the graveyard where his tombstone proclaims

"Cast a cold eye On Life, On Death. Horseman, pass by!",

are all signs of the evanescence of his dream.

The running craze, emanating from America, hit Ireland particularly hard, with around 350 ten-kilometre charity runs and marathons staged in 1985. Although it has declined from a peak of 11,000 entrants, the Dublin City Marathon, with 6,000 entrants in 1985, remains one of the biggest events of its kind in Europe.

Preceding pages:

Pat O'Connor's 1983 film **Ballroom of Romance**, based on a bleak short story by Irish-born author William Trevor which was intended as a harsh reflection on pre-1960 rural Ireland, paradoxically sparked off some new interest in ballrooms and formal dancing. This Sunday night gathering at the Warwick Hotel, Salthill, near Galway, is called Ballroom of Romance. The band which plays there, the Tony Chambers Band – a group made up of Tony Chambers and his two sons – is the band that played in the film and has since also taken its name. The band's foxtrots, quicksteps and waltzes and Tony Chambers's own dramatic vibrato on the saxophone have now been heard far from their small-town base in Newport, County Mayo.

The revival of interest in ballroom music has hardly affected young people. At the Warwick Hotel dances, the 200 who attend each Sunday are mostly middle-aged. But Tom Greaney, a loyal supporter of the Chambers band, believes they exercise a positive influence. "I wish we had more of that," he said. "People would be happier."

The variety of flora which thrives in Ireland's damp, moderate climate — a total of over 900 native species — has made it a happy hunting ground for botanists. In a few square feet of this rough pasture there are white yarrow, black knapweed, vetch and tall oat grass.

This kind of wild, profuse growth is found particularly where the nature of the land makes it difficult to practise a more productive agriculture with intensive grazing.

Following page:

Even in August, the coal was being delivered (left) in Craigavon, the new town between Lurgan and Portadown in County Armagh. Some householders were laying up their stocks for the winter; others were already using it to keep warm on the cold, wet August days.

Craigavon was named after the first prime minister of Northern Ireland, Sir James Craig, later Viscount Craigavon, whose name was also bestowed on the principal bridge linking the east and west sides of Derry. The Lion of Craigavon's promise of 20 years ago, when construction of Ireland's second new town — second to Shannon — began, has faded fast. Over one quarter of the 4,000 houses built in the past two decades are empty. Some of the newly built estates have never been occupied. The trumpeted jobs have not materialised and people who moved out of Belfast have moved back in again.

The new town has an unemployment rate of 22%. And self-employment, as in coal deliveries, or other door-to-door sales, have become a last hope for many who lost their jobs.

For John Reilly, of County Leitrim, coal is his life. He works in the pit at Arigna, County Roscommon, where he is seen taking his mid-morning break. This is one of the few occasions when the miners can mingle while at work — even if it is under the light of their own lamps. For most of the time they work alone and in almost complete darkness.

JAKE WALLIS

MIKE ABRAHAMS

extended his operations to Mosney, County Meath in Ireland, a few years after the end of the Second World War. Mosney is a short trip north of Dublin on the main railway line and is also easily accessible from Belfast. In the 1960s it became popular with working-class Catholic holiday-makers from Northern Ireland, as well as with Dubliners.

The Mosney camp maintained all the features of the British holiday camps – communal living, organised games and competitions, and cabaret entertainment laid on.

With the increased availability of cheap package holidays to the sun, Mosney passed its heyday. But a local entrepreneur, Phelim McCloskey, has revitalised it in recent years. These old people were brought to the camp for a week's holiday by the charitable Lions Club, a fund-raising organisation run by businessmen.

Following pages:

On a normal Saturday morning in the centre of Crossmaglen, County Armagh, a farmer with his bicycle is talking to a townswoman, the post is being delivered, a child holds a balloon and one of the dozen daily foot patrols which make forays from the British Army post on the edge of the town reminds people that normal life here is not so normal after all. "Cross" has a population of just over 1,500, is situated within a couple of miles of the border with the Republic and has attained international fame as a symbol of the IRA's continued military campaign against the British Army.

Earlier in August a delegation from Irish Northern Aid, a republican support group in the United States, was taken here. Crossmaglen was quieter in that month than it had been for many Augusts. An IRA mortar attack on the army post, which occupies the Gaelic football field, failed.

MARTIN PARR

OPTIONS

What Makes
Some People Better
To Work With
Than Live With?

Is Erotic Exotic?
Read All About It

TOM KELLY

Rising out of the rebuilt Bogside district of Derry is Limewood Street, where in recent years – and despite the "Troubles" – houses have been improved and kitchens, bathrooms, and bedrooms built on to make more space. Like other Irish towns with a historically important industrial base, Derry has many streets of terraced housing and where, now, that industrial base (in Derry's case, shirt-making) is a faint memory. Even with the establishment of new industries on the outskirts of the city, Derry is one of the unemployment "black spots" of Britain and Ireland, with 38% jobless among adult males.

In November, the multi-national Dupont, with a factory at Maydown just outside Derry, announced an investment of £45 million in an additional plant making a new synthetic fibre and employing up to 300 people.

Preceding pages:

Money and religion have always co-existed in Knock, County Mayo (right), ever since the Virgin Mary and a group of attendant saints made an appearance in the tiny village during the land wars of the last century. Monsignor James Horan, parish priest of Knock, has managed to embody both God and Mammon for his parishioners, building the shrine into a tourist attraction and a place of worship.

Monsignor Horan has a legendary reputation, built on such incidents as the reported sighting of the devil at the dance hall in Tooreen, County Mayo, where he used to run regular dances in the 1950s. Some say the story was spread by Albert Reynolds, former Fianna Fáil minister, in order to drive the dancers away and towards a nearby ballroom of his own. Others say it was Monsignor Horan who spread the story as an extra attraction.

The Monsignor's legend is justified by two extraordinary achievements – attracting Pope John Paul II to the remote village to celebrate the centenary of the apparition in 1979; and raising the money – most of it from the government – to build an airport on a hilltop a few miles from Knock. The first international pilgrim flight was serviced there in October 1985 – the flight was *leaving* Knock for Rome.

As always, the business follows the custom. Tony Weldon's new Cut'n'Shape hairdressers in Tallaght Town Centre, Dublin (left), is evidence of the new thrust to service the sprawling housing estates of south west Dublin, originally built without shopping or entertainment facilities and even now hardly resembling the "new town" that they were supposed to comprise.

SYD SHELTON

Patrick Kelly lives with his best friends in the kitchen/living room/bedroom of his cottage at Mullaghmore, County Sligo.

Mr Kelly is virtually – and untypically – self-sufficient on his small holding, even growing rye for straw to thatch his roof. He has a second house in the seaside village of Mullaghmore, which he rents to summer visitors while he returns to the frugal, familiar surroundings of the older home. Tens of thousands of single farmers over 60 lead a very poor life on small holdings, with no hope of making them viable nor any immediate relative to help them or take over the farms.

Preceding pages:

The creeper had reclaimed the many-turreted ruin of Baldwinstown Castle long before 1985 when the 800-year association of one family with the south County Wexford castle came to an end. Four sisters who had lived in an 18th century house beside the castle ruin were the last representatives of the Norman family of Stafford which established itself here in the 12th century. Expelled from their property by the Cromwellians in the mid 17th century, the Staffords later bought back the family seat.

Within months of the last Stafford resident dying, their nephew in the United States sold the 60 acres, plus house, plus ruin, to a local farmer. Friesian cows (right) make up the vast majority of the two million dairy cattle in Ireland. And the black plastic sheeting and the tyres which cover the silage they are eating have become as distinctive a feature of the Irish countryside as the black-and-white cows.

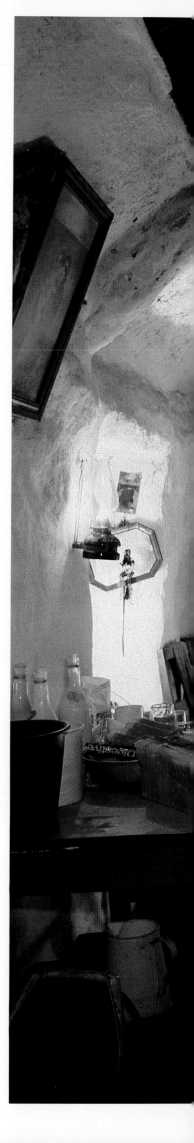

GERAY SWEENEY

RED SAUNDERS

TOM KELLY

The door is shut at McCarthy's of Castletownshend, in west County Cork, where the Cork-brewed stout, Murphy's, takes precedence over the better-known rival, Guinness, from Dublin.

Pubs are often part-time, shared with the running of a farm or a family, with selling property or livestock.

Alongside the brasher "lounges", these are places for quiet reflection but, in the winter, when there is little passing trade, they can be lonely, dim-lit refuges.

Castletownshend is a slow-moving, well-mannered village, which bears the marks of its long domination by the Big Houses.

Preceding pages:

Seagulls, not pigeons, are the native bird of Dublin city. Since the Vikings appeared on the River Liffey in 837 AD, the river has shaped the city. In **Finnegan's Wake** James Joyce used the goddess of the river, Anna Livia, to personify the city as it wanders "from swerve of shore to bend of bay".

The life that flowed up and down the river, with ships sailing right up into the city centre and barges hauling beer down to the docks from the huge Guinness brewery upriver, kept Dublin open to the world.

James Gandon's Custom House on the riverside (right, background), is one of the city's finest buildings from the classical Georgian period and a monument to its trading tradition. Hector Grey's Sunday morning street auctions held by the Halfpenny Bridge (foreground) represented another side of that tradition.

The port itself has moved almost entirely out onto land reclaimed from Dublin Bay. Only a few small ships dock within sight of the city centre and a new road bridge keeps them at a distance.

At Wood Quay, the site of the first settlements by the Vikings who founded the city, the huge bunker-like Civic Offices (left), new headquarters for Dublin Corporation, have been built after years of opposition and mass demonstrations by those anxious to maintain the heritage intact. At over £20 million, the two blocks are the most expensive buildings ever erected in Dublin, costing ten times the original estimate given in 1967.

Their design was the work of Dublin's best-known and most controversial architect, Sam Stephenson.

The image of Our Lady of Lourdes sits easily beside a take-away food shop in Rathnew, County Wicklow. Since the Feast of Our Lady of Lourdes was established by Pope Pius X in 1907, and more particularly since the launch of cheap packaged pilgrimages to the shrine, Lourdes has had an important place in popular religion in Ireland. This grotto was erected in 1979, when the visit to Ireland of Pope John Paul II led to an upsurge of religious fervour.

Meadow, Mountain And Sea

It is worth asking why, having walked across from the mainland about 7,000 years ago, the first settlers should have decided to remain in Ireland; and why others should have followed them, even though shortly afterwards the sea rose sufficiently to make a hazardous crossing in primitive boats necessary. There cannot, after all, have been any great pressure of population in mainland Europe, even for mesolithic food gatherers; and though its summers may have been one or two degrees warmer then than now, climatic conditions in the new island were basically the same as those which the present day inhabitants spend their lives bemoaning.

The early settlers would have found a well-wooded island, with forests of oak, elm, pine and hazel and plenty of bog as well as many inviting river valleys and reed-fringed lakes. As others have done since –

although nobody may in the future – these first inhabitants would have found the fishing to be good; and, as they penetrated very slowly into the island from the north-east, they settled beside the numerous stretches of water.

On investigation (which of course took a very long time) these first inhabitants would have found that the island they now lived in was bowl-shaped, with a large, ill-drained, central plain or valley and mountains mostly around the edge. The slopes of these mountains, being wooded, did not present the same outline as today; but the sky behind them was the same, so were the tumultuous cloudscapes, and so was the ever-changing, moisture-laden light, sometimes reducing everything to monotones, sometimes magically enhancing colour, sometimes, particularly in early summer, giving a blue effect quite near at hand, as if the whole island had been raised almost into the sky. The intense greenness, which never fails to startle travellers from hotter, drier lands and is nostalgically lamented in so many songs of exile, would not have been a year-round phenomenon then, for in October and November the forest would have flamed with the colours of autumn, but it would have been there for much of the time and so would have been the juxtaposition of green landscape with grey, over-hanging sky.

These early settlers probably spent a good deal of their waking hours in the open air; and whatever garb they wore they would have noted something else: the Irish climate permitted you to be out for most of the year without serious affliction. Indeed if they had known much about the other climates of the world they might have agreed that one could be out of doors for more days of the year without discomfort in Ireland than any place else in the world except the neighbouring island.

It was Friedrich Engels who said that the climate of Ireland was a political matter. In his day debate raged about whether that climate made it possible, profitable or desirable to raise a variety of crops or whether it would be better to turn the whole place into grassland for the raising of beef cattle. Since the economic self-interest of the landlords and larger farmers dictated the latter course, learned opinion naturally favoured it also.

At the time of the mesolithic food gatherers even the lush grasslands were in the future, but they would certainly have observed the luxuriance of the vegetation and the ease with which everything grew in the warm, moist air. When the first farmers came about 3,500 years ago (or perhaps one should say, when the natives took to farming, for there is no warranty for assuming that all technological innovation was the result of invasion) they proceeded to make clearances with surprising rapidity; and though the climate was a little warmer and drier then than it had been or is now, they must have noted the speed with which the green grass grew as well as – to revert to the argument of Engels's time – how readily wheat, barley and other crops could be raised.

There were thus three reasons why people should want to live in Ireland: its fertility, its pleasant climate and its natural beauty. For the very earliest inhabitants the question of mineral deposits, the famous "natural resources" of the first industrial revolution, was not important, and though the absence of coal and other substances bulked large in the geography textbooks of the earlier years of this century (textbooks where Ireland was concerned always compared it to England and always to its disadvantage) it does not seem so important now either.

Probably the sheer bountifulness of the island mattered most to the first Irish. Like the farmers of today, except in exceptional years they would have recognised the plentiful rainfall as for the most part a blessing, not a curse. But though we should not underestimate the wisdom of the first farmers they probably did not know that the ease with which cattle could be reared or crops raised was largely due to the limestone drift which the glaciers of the ice age had crushed into the soil and to the bed of limestone which underlies so much of the country.

Of course, there was and is a good deal of bog – almost a quarter of the whole – and a good deal of barren mountain moorland. The bog has been mechanically exploited in recent times and the moor is being planted with coniferous forest, so they are not such liabilities as the geographers of a former age thought. And for modern men and women – a species which, contrary to some reports, does exist in Ireland – they provide that contrast between carefully tended, pastoral landscapes and wilder, emptier and more primitive ones, between the idea of man as cultivator and shaper and man as a small being confronting larger forces, which strikes the traveller everywhere. It is only a little over one hundred miles from the rich pastures of the Golden Vale in County Tipperary to the wild moorlands of Connemara; far less than that from the meadows of the Slaney valley to the beautiful desolation of the Glen of Imaal.

And this is a fact that brings us to something else about Ireland and the relationship of its inhabitants to the land where their lot is cast. From a very early stage they were conscious of living on an island. The authors of the prehistoric sagas on which the Irish imagination fed knew its mountains and its river valleys, its lush pastures and its grey lakes; and they took the whole place for the domain of their gods and heroes. Islands, perhaps because they have set and easily reached limits, do take a strong grip on the imaginations of those who dwell in them. Certainly this one does, as its history and literature, its songs and oral traditions all amply prove.

JAKE WALLIS

The sight and sound of water, falling and flooding, filled the last days of August 1985. Rivers were at winter levels, hillsides were soggy under foot and streams which might in other summers have been no more than trickles were flowing strongly. This waterfall tumbles down from hills on the border of counties Cork and Kerry, near the town of Kenmare. This is "coom" country, where glaciers cut seat-shaped hollows (cooms) in the hills, where a nearby peak is called Coomnadiha and a lake is called Lough Coomnalach.

And there are more mellifluous names for the mountains — Knockagorraveela and Maulnagowna. But the place-names also echo history. The waterfall flows into Inchiquin Lough, which bears the name of the powerful O Quins. The family's spread is reflected in the place-name, Inchiquin, which recurs in counties Cork, Clare and Galway.

Preceding pages:

In bad years, the saving of the hay goes on into late August. It was a bad year. And when the hay was saved, it was a worse year.

The cocks are tied down with string, weighted with stones, and left in the fields to season before being moved into the haybarn.

This time, they never got that far.

JOHN CLARIDGE

Ireland's raised bogs are a source of fuel for tens of thousands of families in the Midlands and West who have "turbary rights" to pieces of bog. They are a source of fascination to botanists, including the British television personality and conservation campaigner, David Bellamy, for their unique flowers and grasses. And they are a source of fun for sportsmen who shoot the wide range of game birds who find the bogs a congenial habitat.

Following pages:

An oil drum washes ashore on the isolated beach at Loughros Point, County Donegal, a careless greeting from a passing ship or trawler. But hundreds of miles of long west coast beaches facing the Atlantic remain free of any risk of serious pollution. On the less exposed east coast, where there is less movement in the water and the population is denser, the pollution hazard is less visible than an oil drum. Untreated or inadequately treated sewage is carried back on to beaches near Dublin. The capital city's unique location between hills and sea gave it an amenity in the bay; its rapid growth has qualified the value of that amenity.

EDDIE KULIGOWSKI

In the 17th century, one of Oliver Cromwell's generals remarked of the Burren, an area of 50 square miles of bare limestone terraces, that "there is not water enough to drown a man, wood enough to hang him, nor earth enough to bury him".

Yet this inhospitable-looking landscape gives shelter both to man, who has constructed dry-stone walls in an attempt to make the land workable, and to a startling collection of wild flora, many of them rare. The megalithic tomb at Poulnabrone is itself evidence of that tenacity of humanity's mark on this landscape, having been constructed around 4000 years ago. But even its name — the hole of the mill stone — relates to the rocks.

There are reckoned to be 151 portal dolmens of this type in Ireland, some with 20-ton rocks balanced even more precariously on stone pillars. Their precise origins and the methods by which they were erected are the subject of speculation. Similar tombs are found in the western-most parts of continental Europe.

Following pages:

By late August it was reckoned that two-thirds of the intended crop of hay (or one million acres) were lost. Farmers were encouraged to make silage, bringing in contractors (at £40 an acre) to crop the grass green and finely chopped, as an alternative winter fodder.

These fields in County Westmeath (left) were harvested for silage during "a massive turn to silage" which prompted about one-tenth of all farmers to apply for new government grants to assist them as first-time silage makers.

As the weather improved in the following two months, some of the previously uncut hay was "saved" — uniquely, as late as the end of October. Some went for late silage; more was stored as hay, most was poor quality as either. But the controversy about the appropriate remedies — grain or cash — for farmers deprived of adequate winter feed rumbled on.

In a County Wexford field (right) much of the grain was 'lodged' (beaten down) by rain but at least there were bales of straw to be won.

BARRIE ROKEACH

The road rises from Ardara, County Donegal, over the hills towards the fishing port of Killybegs, branching off up the spectacular Glengesh Pass. The granite hills are bare, with a look of recent eruption. Clumps of trees around the houses provide the only shelter.

Shaggy sheep roam freely in the hills. And in Ardara their wool is hand-woven into traditional tweeds, now finding a place in the international fashion market-place. In the scattered cottages, hand-knitters work on the heavy *báinín* jerseys which are distinctly Donegal.

The spinning, knitting and weaving are strongly supported by the state-owned Udarás na Gaeltachta, the development authority for the Irish-speaking areas.

Following pages:

The Aran islands (left) may not have had their first inhabitants for many centuries after the first populations were established in the eastern coastal plains. But the relics of those early Aran islanders who lived in these inhospitable places 3,000 years ago are still clearly visible. Nine dry-stone forts including the unusually well preserved ring fort, Dun Aengus, on the largest island, Inishmore, are counted among the finest prehistoric forts in western Europe.

The islands also have dolmens from the same period and remains of Christian buildings — beehive huts, oratories and small churches — which date back as far as those anywhere else in Ireland.

Large parts of the islands consist of great slabs of stone, an extension of the carboniferous limestone structures of the Burren in County Clare.

The Aran islands stand at the entrance to Galway Bay with two lighthouses, one on Inishere to the south, and one on the rock island, Eireach, seen here, to the north, warning passing ships to keep their distance.

The reeds (right) at the shore of one of the many inland lakes which dot the Midlands counties of Monaghan, Cavan, Leitrim, Longord and Westmeath are part of a rich natural environment which is increasingly under threat from silage and slurry and from local authority sewage wastes. The often half hidden lakes are sought out particularly by English and continental European coarse anglers in pursuit of the pike.

JAKE WALLIS

ALEN MACWEENEY

The ancient forests of Ireland gave the massive bogs. But the country seems remarkably free of trees, except for the random growth of hedges. Hills rising only a few hundred metres above sea level stand bare. Old natural forests of oak are rare – and threatened. Disease has decimated the population of elm trees.

In the last 30 years, however, state forests have been planted on over 400,000 hectares in the Republic, with another 10,000 hectares being added each year. Afforestation has been more intensive in the North. Virtually all of the new plantations are spruce and pine, growing fast and already yielding a harvest for a skeletal timber industry, for chipboard, pulp, construction timber, fencing posts and boxwood.

Here in the valley of the river Suir, near Clonmel, County Tipperary, with the grasslands below, some of the 20-year-old forest has been felled and more has been taken down by the force of falling trees or by the wind. Despite generous incentives, private forest plantations have developed slowly. And even in those parts of the country where the land is too poor to support a viable agriculture, there is continuing resistance to afforestation.

Farmers hold firmly to their fields as the odds rise against their being put to productive farming use.

The sea may have claimed some of them. The town of Burtonport, near this church at Kincasslagh, has sometimes been stilled for days by a trawler tragedy. Now Boyles, Gallaghers and McGinleys have come to rest where the Rosses district of County Donegal meets the sea. For some, the burial will also have been the occasion of their return home from Glasgow or Boston, favoured targets of Donegal emigrants.

Following pages

There were few people on the long, unspoiled beach at Silver Strand, Thallabawn, County Mayo. It stands exposed to the unrelenting force of Atlantic winds and surf. This paradise for surfers (the European surfing championships were held later in the year in neighbouring County Sligo) only lacks the sun of other more favoured west coasts.

EDDIE KULIGOWSKI

Evening sinking into the Atlantic softens the harsh, unrelenting grey of the Burren in County Clare. It is both in fact and in name a rocky district, with a peculiar other-worldly aura. Here, at Doolin Point, the unbroken line of rock and cliff off north-west Clare yields a little – but only a little, for the sandy beach at Doolin is treacherous. In August 1983, it claimed the lives of eight young people who sought relief from the sweat of an open-air music festival.

Following pages:

Climbing sheer and grey for nearly 200 metres out of the Atlantic Ocean, the cliffs of Moher wind for 8 kilometres along the coastline of County Clare. Colossal troughs of rock loop into a spectacular row of coves. Herring gulls fleck the skies for these cliffs are both nesting-place and resting-place for vast flocks of seabirds. Kittiwakes and guillemots share the same narrow cliff-ledges; razor-bills and puffins cling to the damp rockface. And every tourist coach stops and snaps the view.

JOHN CLARIDGE

JOHN CLARIDGE

TOM KELLY

BARRIE ROKEACH TOM KELLY

The lighthouse at Poolbeg, at the end of the south Bull Wall, marks the entrance to Dublin harbour. For nearly 200 years, keepers lived in the buildings beside it. In the late 1960s, the lighthouse, built in 1768 and the oldest in Dublin, was automated.

The port of Dublin developed in the early 18th century along the north side of the River Liffey, later along the south quays. The two Bull Walls, tapering towards the port entrance and regarded as "a brilliant piece of engineering", were built later again to ensure a flow of water which would prevent the build up of sediment at the mouth of the harbour.

The Bull Walls also provide a valued amenity – for Sunday strollers and for everyday swimmers who come here to the Half Moon Swimming Club.

Preceding pages:

The Hill of Tara (top left) where a statue of Ireland's patron saint, Patrick, recalls the visit of the first Christian missionary to the court of the High King.

Tara was for centuries the political centre of Ireland; the trace of the extensive 1500 year-old court can still be seen on the hill which commands views in all directions over the rich lands of County Meath.

The hedgerows of hawthorn, bramble, elder and ash (bottom left) hold the mist down in the fields of the Midlands as the day struggles through.

From the mouth of the river Liffey, looking northwards, the view is of the Hill of Howth sheltering the bay (top right). From the sand-dune Bull Island – where migratory geese from the Arctic Circle mingle with city golfers – the twin stacks of the power station at Poolbeg now a familiar part of the landscape (bottom right).

Samuel Richard Grubb, High Sheriff
of County Tipperary, left instructions
that he was to be buried standing up
so that from this point he could, like
Moses, "view the landscape o'er", as
his favourite hymn-writer put it. He
died in 1921 and his grave on the side
of the hill near the Vee Gap in the
Knockmealdown mountains is
marked by a cairn (mound) of stones.
From there the prospect is of County
Tipperary's green fields stretching
away to the Galtee mountains
(left background).
The Grubb family came to Ireland as
Anabaptists in the mid-17th century,
and soon became Quakers. They
have lived, as Samuel Grubb did, at
Clogheen, in the County Tipperary for
200 years. It is from Clogheen that
the Vee road winds up the hillside to
350 metres above sea level and falls
from there into the wooded valleys of
east County Waterford.
On Sunday, 26th August, the tanker
from Mitchelstown Creamery called
to Denis O'Brien's farm, close to the
border of Counties Tipperary and
Cork, later than on other days.
The O'Brien family was just about to
go to mass.

Every morning, throughout the
country, large tankers brush either
side of small roads as they collect
milk from dairy farmers who have
now widely acquired their own
storage and cooling facilities.
The creameries are owned
co-operatively by farmer-
shareholders, but run aggressively as
big businesses, often in competition
with one another, for milk supplies.
They are among Ireland's largest and
technically most advanced
companies. And Mitchelstown has
the largest sales of any dairy co-op.
One creamery makes alcohol from
milk, another makes feta cheese for
export to the Middle East, another
rigato cheese for export to Italy. And
the original Irish cream liqueur,
blending cream and whiskey, was
developed by a co-operative
creamery in County Cavan. It has
been flattered by being imitated
widely – and not just in Ireland.

PETER LAVERY

At Mary Fyffe's home at Fallinlea, there is plenty of room to hang out the washing. From there, the view is across Glenariff to Carn Neil mountain, 340 metres high and looking out to the Scottish coast. This is one of the nine glens of Antrim in the north-east. Glenariff – the valley and the river in it have the same name – runs down to the sea and to the spectacular Antrim coast road at the village of Waterfoot. The land is poor, used mainly for grazing sheep and cattle. Here, in a space bordered by the strongly loyalist districts of Larne and Ballymena, traditions of Gaelic Ireland – albeit with a strong Scottish flavour – survived more vigorously than in other parts of colonised Ulster.

On Monday, 26th August, the Ould Lammas fair, held both for selling and for celebration of the harvest took place at Ballycastle on the north Antrim coast. The people of the glens brought their stock down for sale to be greeted by travelling traders offering cheap rugs and blankets. Lammas Day was originally on 1st August and the fair held on 12th August when loyalist Ulster was commemorating the Siege of Derry. The date has been re-arranged to coincide with a more recently established Bank Holiday.

TOM KELLY

Cloonee Lough, County Kerry, the bare, barren beauty of the hills, moors and lakes of the west of Ireland has become a "typical" Irish landscape. But the many hundreds of lakes which pock-mark the countryside across the north Midlands offer a different, friendlier aspect. Some were chosen as sites for dwellings by early Irish inhabitants of over 3,000 years ago. Others have been places of meditation and pilgrimage for 1,000 years. And more have been happy hunting grounds for anglers and naturalists, as well as, in more recent years, boaters and surfboarders.

Preceding pages:

The islands off the west coast of Ireland are losing their people steadily. The Blasket islands off County Kerry (right) are no longer inhabited.

An occasional visitor to the Blasket Islands during August was Charles Haughey, leader of the Fianna Fail party, who built a home on Inishvickillane, the southern-most Blasket, transporting materials by helicopter and boat. Mr Haughey also brought in deer which have been breeding successfully on the island.

The Blaskets have had no permanent population for over 30 years, although some of the former inhabitants living on the nearest part of the mainland still fish around the islands or graze sheep on them. The last two generations of islands produced a unique literature in the few decades after the first of them learned to read and write. Tomas O Crohan, Maurice O'Sullivan, Michael O'Guiheen and Peig Sayers are among the authors of a distinguished library of a dozen books of stories and reminiscences – in Peig Sayers's case, recorded and transcribed by her son.

English scholars, Robin Flower and George Thomson, were fascinated by this highly cultured island people. Robin Flower was a regular visitor from 1910 taking down tales from Tomás O Crohan and encouraging him to write.

George Thomson underlined the Blasket islanders' unique achievement remarking that they had ''no priest, no pub, no police'' but had committed their lore and their harsh experience to writing themselves, rather than having others do it for them.

Doo Lough (left), is narrow, deep and bleak. Here in South County Mayo there are no villages, few houses, few trees, just a lot of bog and a lot of sheep.

From the peak of Slieve League at 1972 feet above sea level, the land falls steeply into the sea. Access to the summit is on the One Man's Pass, starting at the Eagle's Nest above this inlet at Bunglass, near the village of Teelin, in south-west Donegal.

As always in these inaccessible places – or so it seems – there is the ruin of an early Christian church near the top of the cliff face.

TOM KELLY

The People, The Politics, The Power

To a greater extent than in any other European country, the pattern of Irish politics, north and south, is historically determined. The student enquiring into the differences between the two major political parties in the Republic, Fianna Fáil (The Warrior Band of Destiny) and Fine Gael (The Tribe of the Irish) is referred to a split in the ranks of insurgent Irish nationalism which took place in 1922 and was occasioned by some fairly minor provisions of the Anglo-Irish agreement or "treaty" of that year.

There is little difference in social policy between them, the student is told. When in power both of them are victims or beneficiaries of the international economic situation, whatever it may be. Both take advice from the same civil servants in the Departments of Finance, Industry and Agriculture. Both pander to foreign investment. Both are fearful of offending the Catholic Church.

But one is slightly more nationalist than the other. That is why they split and formed themselves into separate parties in the first place. When there are differences with Britain over Northern Ireland policy or over Irish rights generally, Fianna Fáil, whose founders objected to the taking of a purely ritual and symbolic oath of allegiance to a British king in 1922, presents a slightly stiffer front than does Fine Gael. Or, to put it the other way round, Fine Gael is slightly fonder of Britain than Fianna Fáil.

And north of the border the attitudes of political parties have their roots even deeper in history. The nationalist (Catholic) parties represent those who have a sense of dispossession in their own land; and the unionist (Protestant) parties those whose original title or perhaps mere presence in the island derived from the British conquest.

Yet it is probably true to say that, north or south of the border, a degree of nationalism implies a degree of social radicalism, however confused, while unionism or pro-British sentiment implies a degree of conservatism. Besides pure green nationalism there is, after all, a nationalism of the dispossessed, which nearly always discolours or tinges the purer colouration with something else. And Britain was, for eight centuries, the stable, big-power factor in the Irish situation, the upholder of the law, such as it was, and the enforcer of all property rights deriving from that law. So those who have a sense of grievance, who have something to gain or regain, tend to be nationalist; those who have something to lose tend to be pro-British: Fianna Fáil has a history of mild social radicalism as well as mildly radical nationalism. When the founders of Fine Gael signed the treaty in 1922, they appealed to all those who had a "stake in the country" to support them. Although both parties respect big business, Fianna Fáil appeals more to the go-getters, the get-rich-quick entrepreneurs; while Fine Gael prefers respectability and rectitude. In the Six Counties shades of nationalism are now clearly matched by degrees of commitment to social change, from Sinn Féin's adoption of the socialist workers' republic as its ultimate objective through the social democracy of the SDLP to classical unionism's classically blue conservative stance.

Of course, what surprises most observers is the fact that when Irish politics generally are weighed in the balance, the conservative side so far outweighs any other; but the reason is not really very far to seek. Besides the nationalism of the dispossessed, there is also an ethnic nationalism, deriving its strength, as well as its occasional fury or desperation, from the sense of being ethnically or culturally threatened by an outside force. For many centuries the native Irish felt – and were – culturally threatened linguistically, religiously and otherwise. At certain extreme moments they felt they were being threatened with genocide.

But now, by an irony of history, the descendants of the Scots Protestants whom Britain implanted in the north east in the 17th century, feel these things too — culturally, religiously, now even linguistically threatened. And in border areas they too speak of genocide.

In a country where various groupings have stiffened in attitudes of resistance to threat it is no wonder that when extremes meet in conflict they are as likely to be conservative extremes as conservative and radical ones. In the early days of the present conflict in the north east even the IRA was a conservative force, cherishing certain conservative attitudes to culture and morality.

And it need be no surprise either that there are often confusing and seemingly irreconcilable strands in the same movement. There are extreme Irish nationalists who, in so far as they know anything about them, fear the 200-year-old, liberal, rational, internationalist and egalitarian principles of the French Revolution as posing a threat to the Gaelic, Catholic and hierarchical cultural tradition with which they identify. Yet they call themselves "republicans" and revere Wolfe Tone, who introduced these principles into Ireland, because it was he who also enunciated the doctrine of a complete separation from England, achieved, if needs be, by force, and that is what "republicanism" has come to mean. There are people of a fairly progressive, liberal disposition in the North who support unionist policies because they fear the obscurantist-Catholic, Gaelic-chauvinist elements in Irish nationalism.

Partly because they are rooted in history, however, Irish political parties have a strong binding power. In the south adherence to one or other of the major parties is, in rural areas at least, largely an hereditary matter. Policies change slightly but loyalties do not; and quite a small percentage swing is regarded as significant. A cynical observer might say that this does not matter, since there is so little difference in social policy between them; both admit the helplessness of Ireland's open economy in face of world trends — indeed both are glad to assert it as an alibi — and both favour foreign investment as a means to economic salvation. Neither is willing to give offence to the sort of rural Catholicism which for many voters is still, subconsciously at least, an integral part of their distinctively Irish identity.

It is said that people get the politics they deserve. Given the strength of the party system in most western style democracies, it might be truer to say that people get the sort of politics their ancestors deserved or, at least, thought desirable. In Ireland's case this form of historical determinism is made more powerful by the continued existence of unresolved questions of national identity. The catch is that efforts to resolve them seem only to result in more of the same kind of politics, while the failure to resolve them likewise strengthens the status quo.

The 650 workers at the state-owned Irish Steel plant had gone to the brink. But on Monday afternoon, 26th August, seven hours after the government's deadline for a decision on redundancy proposals, they met at the plant – situated on an island in Cork harbour – and approved by over two-to-one a set of proposals they had previously rejected. Returning here to Cobh by ferry from the factory they barely seemed relieved that the threat of closure had been averted.

The steel-rolling company, taken over by the state in 1947, had been making heavy losses for some years, calling repeatedly on the state exchequer and on the steel-glutted European Economic Community for support. When the workers at the plant turned down Labour Court proposals for 115 redundancies, the Minister for Industry, John Bruton, insisted they had only one more chance to save all their jobs.

Irish Steel is on Haulbowline Island, whose name refers to the necessity to haul in by bowline any sailing ships wishing to berth there. A royal dockyard was built on the island in the latter part of the 19th century by convicts held on the neighbouring Spike Island.

Spike was the last British garrison in the Republic – up to 1938. In spring 1985, the Minister for Justice, Michael Noonan, decided to re-open the abandoned military prison on Spike to relieve drastic over-crowding in other gaols. Within months, there were riots on Spike, the most serious on 1st September when prisoners set fire to and broke up large parts of the prison, holding police, army, and prison warders at bay overnight.

DEREK SPEIRS

TOM KELLY

In the insecure schizophrenic world of the new Dublin middle-class, Terry Keane is one of the few stable lodestars of social success. Married to and separated from the High Court judge Ronan Keane, she works as a fashion journalist — her column is called "Style" — but she is as much a part of the trends as a commentator on them.

Dublin's new rich, emerging in the 1960s, has had to flaunt wealth to convince itself and everyone else that the wealth is real. The Mirabeau Restaurant in southside Sandycove, for instance, was sought out because it was especially expensive. It was more important to be seen eating than it was to eat.

With the recession of the 1980s, conspicuous wealth has gone into a mild decline as a fashion, but Terry Keane has kept the flag flying and her daughter, Madeline (left), has acquired the same bravado in her early 20s, writing of the "boring" over-40s as "wrinklies".

Preceding page:

Lord Kilbracken (left) took over the family seat at Killegar on the borders of counties Cavan and Leitrim in 1950 and it has, in his own words, "been deteriorating ever since". He has written over a dozen books on a wide variety of themes, most recently on his experiences as a Royal Navy pilot during World War II and on methods of recognising birds, trees and wild flowers. Killegar, up a long, pot-holed avenue, looking out on the poor land, forests, small lakes and hillocks of County Leitrim, is his home. The Godley family (later Barons Kilbracken) set up there in 1731. By very conscious choice, the third baron is an Irish citizen, deeply involved in local problems of farming and forestry, as he is in those of the Kurds, whom he has championed. In August, Lord Kilbracken was home with his second wife, Susan, and their four-year-old son, Sean.

Also in the literary and intellectually eclectic tradition of those Anglo-Irish who have survived the loss of most of their properties and their privileges without loss of morale, is Desmond Leslie (right), author and composer, who lives at Castle Leslie in County Monaghan.

He is seen here in the extravagant Victorian house's "Blue Room", with a map of France on which he is exploring the "mystical geometry" of the medieval Knights Templar. The Border with Northern Ireland runs along the perimeter of the Leslie property.

GUGLIELMO GALVIN

RED SAUNDERS

By a margin of just three points (0-8
to 0-5) Drumkerrin beat Annaduff to
win the Leitrim county Gaelic football
final at Carrick-on-Shannon on
Sunday, 25th August. The trophy was
presented to team captain John
McPartland, on his team-mates'
shoulders, by Sean Murray (right), a
civil servant and chairman of the
Leitrim County Board of the Gaelic
Athletic Association.

The GAA, which celebrated its
centenary in 1984, organises football,
hurling and handball (a small ball
struck against a wall, rather than a
larger ball thrown into goals)
throughout the 32 Counties. On that
same Sunday, the All-Ireland football
semi-final was being replayed
between counties Kerry and
Monaghan at GAA headquarters in
Croke Park, Dublin. Kerry won the
replay despite having star player Eoin
Liston sent off. Kerry went on to
defeat Dublin in the final.
Leitrim has not progressed that far in
the All-Ireland championships for very
many years. A county with few work
opportunities, it is also finding it hard
to retain some rising players against
the offers of jobs in the United States
coming from Irish-American
businessmen with an active interest
in Gaelic games teams in the US.

Preceding pages:

Noelle Campbell-Sharpe (right) has
been interested in Napoleon ever since
she came across a book about him in
the town of Wexford where she grew
up. His spirit helped her to rise from
clerk-typist to publisher of *Irish Tatler,
Social and Personal* and the business
magazine *Success*, and self-appointed
examplar to the new entrepreneurs.
The toy soldiers, a complete
collection of models of Napoleon's
Irish regiment, were specially made for
her by a toymaker in the South of
France.

More modestly successful are the
Kennedys, Michael and Maria and their
three children Ailbhe, Ciara and Fergal.
They live in The Dunes in the northside
coastal suburb of Portmarnock, an
early 1970s estate of large middle-
class houses.

Michael Kennedy is an insurance
broker; Maria a housewife and mother;
their two eldest children attend the
local Catholic school. The family home
has four bedrooms, with the possibility
of converting another two rooms to
bedrooms as the children get older.

The car is a large Toyota Crown.
Although they are comfortably off,
Michael and Gisson play Gaelic
football and hurling rather than the
more characteristically middle-class
rugby.

FERGUS BOURKE

At the closing of a camera shutter, the children playing around the health centre in Derry's Creggan district, put on balaclavas and stockings. Being a "volunteer" is a game to be acted out.

Bobby Sands became a powerful symbol of the "terrorist" – to some – or the "volunteer" – to others – when he was the first of the ten IRA and INLA hunger-strikers to die in the H-Blocks of Long Kesh (Maze) prison in May 1981.

Bobby Sands is still revered by republicans as an inspiration to their struggle. His poems and songs were published after his death. On his 1984 album, *Ride On,* singer-songwriter, Christy Moore sings two of Sands's songs, one of them with the catch-line, "I Wish I Was Back Home In Derry".

Preceding pages:

Mary and Buttons (left) live with their parents, Chrissy and Johnny Ward, and eight other children, in a caravan on the northern limits of the city of Dublin. The whole family arrived in a car at photographer Fergus Bourke's studio where he more usually portrays well-known personalities for a newspaper series, "Kindred". Within the travelling community, the Wards are well-known personalities, as active members of the recently formed Minceir Misli organisation, through which the most confident travellers fight for their embattled corner. Chrissy Ward's sister, Nan Joyce, became in the 1980s the single best-known traveller, taking up to Supreme Court level her demand on Dublin County Council to provide an alternative site if they wanted her family to move from their present one. She also took the case of Irish travellers on to the streets of Dublin, and into the institutions of the European Community.

The travellers' case was supported early by singer Christy Moore (right) who for many years included Ewan McColl's song "Go, Move, Shift" in his repertoire. The 40-year-old musician from County Kildare, seen with his daughter, Juno, 9, has won unique status as advocate of radical causes and as a folk hero.

Earlier in August, a solo album, *Ordinary Man,* was barred from sale by the High Court because the owners of the Stardust disco in north Dublin, where 48 young people died in a fire in 1981, complained that the words of the song, "They Never Came Home", could prejudice the outcome of over 100 long drawn-out civil actions against them.

JOHN EGAN

Every spring and summer tens of thousands of Protestant loyalists take to the streets in marches which are supposed to assert their loyalty to the British crown and the memory of the Protestant King William of Orange who defeated the Catholic King James at the battle of the Boyne in 1690.

The marches of the summer of 1985 were special demonstrations, aimed at opposing what some Protestant leaders claimed was a plot by Britain and the government of the Republic to force Protestants into a Catholic-dominated united Ireland. "Protestant feet", said the Reverend Ian Paisley, would march in protest all over Ulster. But in September, the Protestant marchers ran into unexpected trouble when they attempted a gratuitous march through the small Catholic enclave in Portadown, County Armagh, a Protestant stronghold. The Royal Ulster Constabulary opposed them and, to the surprise of some commentators, did so in very determined and stubborn fashion. The parades, with their swaggering drummers and baton-twirlers, their huge banners decorated with religious and historical motifs, and their marchers dressed in bowler hats and orange sashes, are colourful, but are viewed by Catholics as aggressive expressions of Protestant supremacy. Up to 70,000 turn out on marches held on 12th July to commemorate King William's victory at the Battle of the Boyne, though numbers have been dwindling in recent years as young people seek new forms of diversion and middle class Protestants turn away from the Orange Order's bigoted and archaic image.

The British Army's headquarters in Northern Ireland is situated at Thiepval Barracks on the outskirts of the mainly Protestant Lisburn, a centre of the linen industry, eight miles south of Belfast. The Barracks takes its name from the place where nearly 6,000 Ulstermen were killed or wounded fighting for Britain in the Battle of the Somme during World War I. That event, in July 1916, has become as potent a symbol for Ulster Protestants of their loyalty to the British empire as the Easter Rising in Dublin three months earlier has been of Irish republican hostility to imperial rule.

The techniques developed by the British Army, and more recently the Royal Ulster Constabulary, to handle demonstrations and combat the 15-year campaign of the Provisional IRA and other republican groups, have been studied by police forces and armies throughout the Western world. Senior police and military officers from Britain, Western Europe and North America have regularly travelled to Northern Ireland to study the use of dogs, of plastic bullets and of surveillance and intelligence methods to monitor and control communities where support for the IRA is strong.

CHARLES TRAUB

Against an orange evening s[ky]
outside Killyglen Orange Hall[,]
County Antrim, Frank Orr beats th[e]
Lambeg drum in honour of Kin[g]
William of Orange, whom Norther[n]
Protestants credit with havin[g]
brought these drums – then know[n]
as "slashers" – from Hollan[d.]
The drums took their present nam[e]
from a tune which took its name fro[m]
a County Antrim town, Lambe[g]
where Frank Orr live[s.]
For 30 of his 39 years, Frank Orr, [a]
plasterer by trade, has been beatin[g]
the Lambeg. In summer 1985 he wo[n]
one or two drumming contests ever[y]
weekend. On this Friday night he wo[n]
the Wilson Memorial Cup presente[d]
by the Killyglen Drumming Clu[b.]
The contests are generally organise[d]
by lodges (local branches) of th[e]
Orange Order. But to take part, th[e]
drummers must belong to a Lambe[g]
drumming association. And there ar[e]
three to choose from[.]
The contests are intended mainly t[o]
evaluate the quality of the drums –
made of goat skin and oak shells –
rather than the skill of the drummers[.]
But on days of high emotion, whe[n]
the Lambeg drummers march wit[h]
the Orange bands, the drummer[s]
show their prowess and commitmen[t]
by crossing their hands as they bea[t]
the drums, keeping this going unt[il]
their wrists blee[d.]

144

Gerry Adams, President of Sinn Féin and elected member of the British Parliament, visits Mimmie Davidson, a resident of West Belfast who is in her 70s and dying of cancer. Since late 1982, Sinn Féin, the political wing of the Provisional IRA, has been contesting elections with some success, in accordance with the policy summarised by Danny Morrison, a leading member, as "the ballot paper in one hand and the armalite in the other". The party has won up to one third of the votes of Northern Ireland nationalists in elections since then.

Gerry Adams unseated veteran politician Gerry (now Lord) Fitt, in the 1983 general election. Adams is the leading figure among the younger, more politically sophisticated and socially radical leadership of Sinn Féin which has steadily won control of what was once a tradition-bound organisation. The new leadership was largely formed and educated in the internment camps established by the British authorities in 1971.

In Gerry Adams's constituency of West Belfast Sinn Féin runs five "advice centres" dealing with issues such as social welfare and housing which were previously regarded as marginal by militant republicans. Much effort is put into having nationalists get their names on the electoral register.

Sinn Féin's radical socialism co-exists without too much difficulty with a strongly Catholic identity.

Following pages:

The street mural has long been used by both sides in Northern Ireland's conflict of loyalties and traditions. This one proclaims the IRA to be Soldiers of Ireland. A possibly childish hand has added a cryptic note of interrogation. Republican murals are regularly obliterated and as regularly restored.

CHARLES TRAUB

a h-eireann

JOHN EGAN

TONY O'SHEA

In Tralee with Fossett's Circus, Aura and Werner – the Guerreros, when they are on the high wire – joined the whole troupe and the extended Fossett family for the christening in the Big Top of Sonya Rose, grand-child of Teddy Fossett, representing the fourth generation of the family's involvement in the circus. The Guerreros, too, come from circus families, she from Portugal and he from Colombia. They married three days after their first meeting in 1983. Aura had been a contortionist but within two weeks had joined Werner on the high wire, without a harness or safety net. The Guerreros stayed with Fossett's for one eight-month season, during which residents in a number of towns objected to the choice of site for the circus, forcing last-minute changes and cancellations. Fossett's, for their turn, objected to the presence in Ireland of a French circus, travelling to the same towns.

In 1987, Fossett's celebrates its centenary. One of its early leading personalities, Doctor Powell, toured the United States in the mid 19th century, working for some years with Colonel William Cody (Buffalo Bill). Cody's roots are said to be in County Tipperary.

Preceding pages:

The expensive and unreliable Dublin public transport system, run by the state company CIE, has prompted a children's street rhyme which goes "You'll never get to heaven on CIE/'Cos CIE is robbery."

At a time when most major European cities were investing in underground railway systems as the primary means of public transport, Dublin's transport planners put their faith in buses. But in a city which has still preserved much of its 18th century streetscape but has a rapidly growing population, the problems of depending on the roads for transport are enormous. The buses rival the weather as a source of complaint among Dubliners.

CIE has introduced computerised Automatic Vehicle Monitoring systems, new green Bombardier buses whose suspension makes a bus ride more like a voyage on stormy seas, and has been trying for two decades to get the badly paid busworkers to agree to one-person operation of double decker buses.

Two bitter disputes hit Dublin city services in 1985; by November the company was threatening to force through one-person operation, whether there was agreement or not. The busworkers had taken further action, this time stopping work on a Friday night in protest against physical attacks on the crews.

PETER LAVE

Airlie Stud, in west County Dublin, was at the forefront of the revival of the Irish bloodstock industry in the mid-1960s. It remains one of Ireland's most successful studs, spreading over 2000 acres and five separate farms.

Tim Rogers built up the multi-million pound business and his widow, Sonia Rogers, seen here with Ela-Mana-Mou, winner of two major English races, before going to stud, now runs it. She is also a director of the bloodstock sales company, Goff's, whose re-launch in the 1970s at a site in the stud country of County Kildare, gave a further boost to the industry.

Airlie Stud does breeding only, unlike its only rival in terms of the size of the business, Coolmore in County Tipperary, where horses are also trained for racing. Airlie and Vincent O'Brien's Coolmore together sponsor one of the Irish "classics", the 2000 Guineas, run at Ireland's most important race track, the Curragh, in County Kildare.

Ela-Mana-Mou, standing at Airlie since 1980, is estimated to earn about £1 million in stud fees annually. Among the other leading stallions which have stood at Airlie and to which mares are brought for breeding purposes, are Vienna, High Hat, Petingo, Atan, and, most successfully of all, Habitat, still much sought after over ten years after being bought by Airlie.

Bloodstock breeding enjoys a very favourable tax regime and is estimated to have earned over £70 million in imports in two decades.

Preceding page:

The Reillys are one of the two traveller families living in the fields on the slopes of the Dublin mountains, away from the spreading suburb of Tallaght where large travellers' encampments have been the focus of confrontations between travellers and settled residents, between travellers' supporters and evicting council officials.

For over 20 years, there have been battles over the siting of camps provided by the local authorities and over the continuing spread around Dublin of unofficial camps. The majority of Ireland's estimated 13,000-plus travellers live on unapproved sites, some in dilapidated caravans and tents, others in large, colourful caravans, but still lacking many basic services.

Their traditional trades no longer have any value. They keep horses and dogs out of nostalgia. Some have found a livelihood in breaking up cars, or laying tarmac. Most are dependents of the state, holding on to their dignity with difficulty.

Much has been written and much has been rumoured about the long and colourful career of Charles Haughey, the leader of Ireland's largest political party, Fianna Fáil, but still he remains an enigma to the Irish, the subject of almost incessant gossip and speculation.

Among the events in his life which mark him for this fascinated interest are a large personal fortune made in the 1960s and a succession of near-fatal accidents by road, aircraft, horse and yacht. Dismissed from his cabinet post in 1970 and subsequently acquitted on charges of importing arms for the use of militant nationalists in the North, he returned to become leader of the party and Taoiseach (prime minister) in 1979, when he led an accident-prone government. With little scope to demonstrate his early decisive and reformist zeal, he none the less continued to display a strong interest in encouraging Irish cultural activity such as financial measures for the support of Irish writers and artists.

Today he survives as party-leader, ebullient and solid, despite a series of attempts by his own party to oust him.

Following pages:

J. J. Mulvey (top left) has kept some of the trim form he had when he was a boxer over 20 years ago. But he has been unemployed for some years since working as a taxi driver. He lives in the Liberties of Dublin, where the terraced cottages built for labourers and brewery workers have recently acquired a certain radical chic.

The late hours of Monday, 26th August, were relatively quiet in the casualty ward of St. James's Hospital, near the Liberties, until a young traveller (bottom left) came in with cuts to his arms. He told hospital staff he had to inflict the injuries on himself to get out of a fight.

The homeless (top and bottom right) were at the centre of a controversy in August over the inducements allegedly offered to them to become "guinea pigs" in a drugs-testing clinic, run within the St. James's Hospital complex. The Simon Community maintains a hostel and a night shelter in the north city centre. Peter Russell (bottom right) is a regular visitor at the shelter where Simon caters for 45 homeless.

The organisation has hostels and shelters in five cities, providing accommodation for a total of 300 homeless in any one night. There are over 3,000 homeless in Ireland but the Simon Community has often faced strong local opposition in its efforts to give them shelter.

RED SAUNDERS

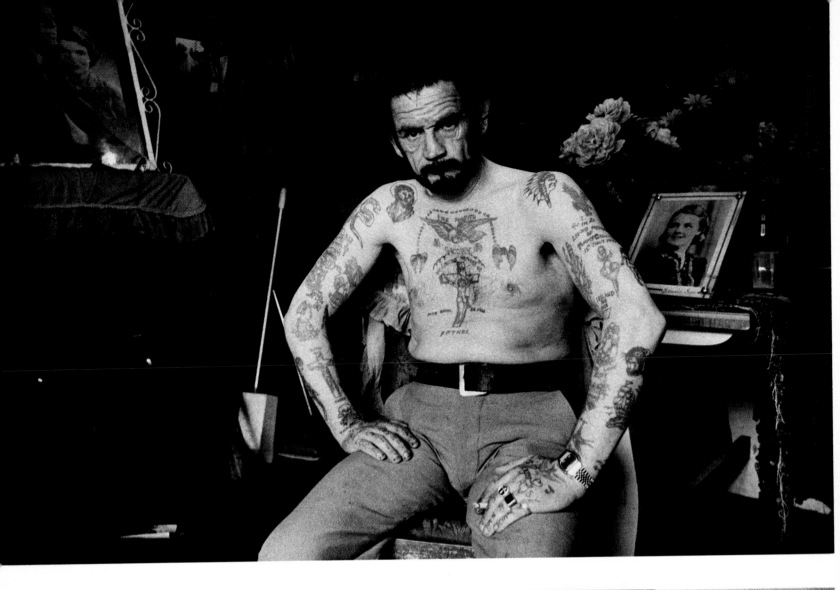
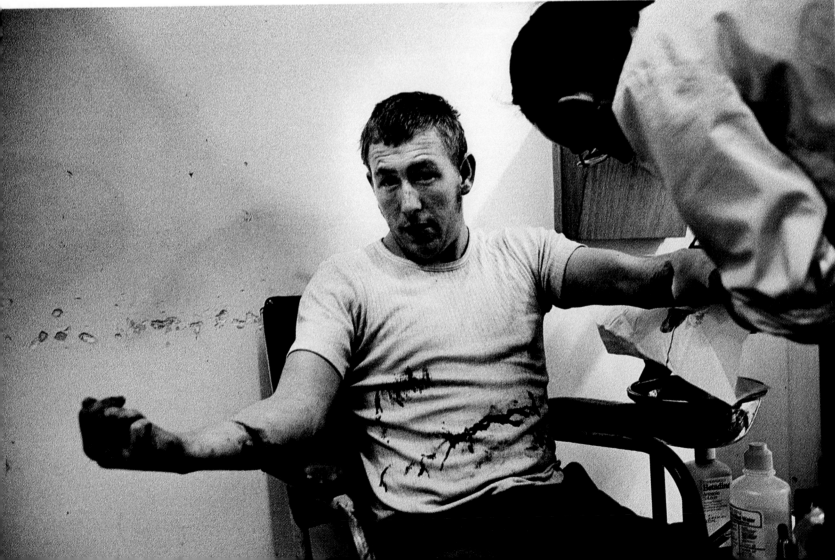

TONY O'SHEA

For some young people living in the countryside, like Matthew Kelly, contact with wild life is immediate, and a fox or a frog represents no great mystery. But as environmentalists become increasingly concerned that the spread of the towns, pollution and changing agricultural practices threaten many species, they have redoubled their efforts to increase young people's awareness of the rich variety of wild life.

"Frogs need shallow, fresh water in which to lay their eggs. In most areas they have become scarce, because of the loss of traditional ponds and poisoning by chemicals. If you know a pond where frogs gather to spawn, try to protect it. Leave the spawn where it is, so that frogs will be back in future years. You can also return to enjoy watching them again — frogs are good fun," advised **Wild Life I**, published for children in autumn 1985.

Following pages:

Images of the smiling Irish colleen (from *cailin*, girl) and of the more serious, remote but beautiful young woman have haunted the romantic poetic imagination — and adorned biscuit tins and bank notes. (In the latter case, it was in Sir John Lavery's painting of his wife, representing Kathleen Ni Houlihan, a personification of Ireland, virgin and unspoiled.)

Ursula Quinn (above) is a 20-year-old student of occupational therapy in a hospital in Dún Laoghaire, near Dublin. She comes from Killybegs, County Donegal, where her father runs an electrical contracting business, and where she returns regularly for holidays with her family. Many thousands of students, civil servants, clerical workers, teachers and nurses — particularly young women — ply a regular route between a flat in Dublin and the larger embrace of the family home in the countryside.

Ireland's largest fishing port, Killybegs, County Donegal (below), was having its worst white fish season for many years — at least, according to the fishermen themselves. But on the weekend of 24th/25th August, the boats were tied up mainly because the skippers were away at an annual golf outing. Those who stayed working at the port were mending nets.

White fish — whiting, cod and plaice — usually keep the trawlers busy between the end of one mackerel season in February and the beginning of another in October. But in summer 1985 it was reported there was "no cod at all"

TOM KELLY

SANDI HABER

TONY O'SHEA

By late August it was clear to the 23 striking night cleaners at University College, Dublin, that they were facing a long and difficult dispute. They struck on 31 July after the contract cleaning company they were working for lost the contract to clean the university buildings and the new contractors declined to take them on. Some of the cleaners had worked there as long as 11 years. In 1982, they had struck for, and won, union recognition. Now they were picketing the college from 6 a.m. (as here) hoping to persuade other groups of contract cleaners to support them. Senior lecturers and administration staff put on gloves and overcoats to clean the buildings affected. And after a 14-week strike, eight of the 15 women who had stuck it out were offered jobs. The rest were given £10,000 to divide between them.

Preceding pages:

The travellers' centre at Exchange House, in a former Dublin Catholic presbytery, was set up to accommodate traveller children who hung around the city centre sniffing glue and sleeping rough at night. The church's contribution of premises was part of its response to the very public and very evident failure of the state services to cater for these children.

The mainstays of the Dublin Committee for Travelling People – formerly, and with a different approach, the Itinerant Settlement Committee – have been a Catholic priest and a leading representative of Ireland's small Quaker community.

Exchange House ceased to be a residential centre when the committee opened another home for girls. Many of their parents had been brought up in care, often then falling prey to alcoholism. A second generation of demoralised travellers is being brought up in institutions.

When Mary Clifford, 4, was taken to the seaside for the first time earlier in the summer, she was so frightened by the sight and sound that she had to be taken home. In August she and her sister, Helen, 15, and the rest of the family, from Callinafercy, Milltown, County Kerry – less than five miles from the sea – had come the 100 miles to Sherkin Island, off south-west Cork. Mary, surrounded by the sea, had made an uncertain peace with it. Here she is sitting on the harbour wall with Helen.

Following pages:

Like many traditional pastimes of the British working-class (English soccer, darts in pubs, fish and chips and football pools), bingo enjoys a continuing popularity in Ireland, particularly on the east coast. This family (left) is anxiously watching the numbers in the amusement arcade in Courtown Harbour, County Wexford.

The family name of O'Farrell used to grace the front of the pub until Ronald Reagan became President of the United States and someone had a close look at the parish register in Ballyporeen. That document "revealed" that Michael, son of Thomas Reagan and Margaret Murphy, was baptised in the local church in September 1829. Thomas went to Illinois, begat John, who begat John Edward, who begat Ronald, who decided to rediscover his Irish roots in June 1984 in the run-up to the presidential election. O'Farrell's pub was burned down by the Black and Tans in the Irish War of Independence in 1922 after two members of that force of British irregular troops were shot on the street outside, but the new pub proved to be considerably more welcoming to the hordes of secret service men with bulging jackets who descended on it during the preparations for the carefully-staged Reagan visit.

The painted O'Farrell sign was replaced with a plastic Ronald Reagan one above the lounge door and plastic sachets of mud from the Reagan ancestral fields are sold for one pound to American visitors. The Reagans visited the pub briefly, posed for the cameras with a pint of beer and left. The President did not in fact drink the pint of Smithwicks. Seen in the poster behind the Reagans are John and Maureen O'Farrell, owners of the pub.

SUE PACKER

President Reagan during his visit here on 3rd June 198 drinking a pint of Smithwick's, Ireland's Nº1 Ale.

PETER LAVERY

CHARLES TRAUB

Members of the Ulster Defence
Regiment — just 15 years old but the
British army's largest, with 6,500
soldiers and officers — prepare to go
on patrol in Belfast (above). All
soldiers brought in from Britain were
gradually withdrawn in the mid 1970s,
the locally recruited and mostly part-
time UDR took over their role.
Up to August 1985, 149 UDR men and
women had been killed, 121 of them
while they were at home or at work.
All but 180 members of the regiment
are Protestants and these killings
have been seen by Protestants as an
attack on their community.
The UDR is disliked by Northern
Catholics even more than the British
Army because of its anti-Catholic
tendency. Young Catholics are
detained at UDR checkpoints, often,
it seems, for no good security
reason. Nearly 40 serving or recently
resigned members of the UDR have
been convicted of "terrorist-type"
crimes, from murder to membership
of illegal para-military groups.
Waterford Street in the Lower Falls
Road area of West Belfast (below) is
one of a group of streets that have
been used frequently as a base for
IRA actions against security targets.
The street is also an officially
designated "development area"
where a house-building programme
has enabled over three-quarters of
the residents to be re-housed since
1976. With the last two phases of the
programme underway, some houses
lie derelict, awaiting demolition.

Preceding pages

In August 1985, exactly 16 years after
the British army was first deployed on
the streets of Belfast, there were
9,000 regular British army soldiers in
Northern Ireland, compared with
21,000 in 1972, the worst year of the
"Troubles", when 467 people,
including over 100 soldiers, died in
violence. In the first eight months of
1985, the death toll in political
violence was one tenth of the 1972
total. Only two British soldiers had
been killed.
Working class Catholic areas of
Belfast and Derry are strongholds of
the Provisional IRA. They are largely
policed by British army foot patrols.
They are transported to their "beat"
and supported by armoured
personnel carriers.
They later retreat behind the
corrugated iron surrounds of hastily
erected barracks, such as Fort
Whiterock.
This soldier, exhausted after a patrol,
is from the First Battalion of the
Green Howards, a Yorkshire regiment
which was then on its eighth tour of
duty in Northern Ireland.

CHARLES TRAUB

MARKETA LUSKACOVA

At the weekly press conference
the Democratic Unionist Party, in t
Stormont building housing t
Northern Ireland Assembly, par
leader Rev. Ian Paisley, member
that assembly, of the House
Commons and of the Europe
Parliament, claimed that it would t
part of the pending Anglo-Iris
Agreement that members of th
Royal Ulster Constabulary be r
longer required to swear an oath
allegiance to the British Crow
The agreement between the Britis
and Irish governments announced
November 1985 included no suc
provision. It established that details
security policy would be discusse
with other matters through an inte
governmental conference with i
secretariat in Stormont. Ian Paisle
and other members of th
Democratic Unionist Party as well a
members of the Official Unioni
Party resigned their seats in th
House of Commons in protes
On the Bank Holiday (below), 26
August, the "county set" of Count
Down, in Northern Ireland, were a
the races in Downpatrick,
racecourse set in polite Protestar
farming country. Candy Devine,
well-known presenter with th
Northern commercial radio statio
Downtown Radio, interviewed "th
best-dressed woman" selected by
panel of judge

Preceding page

On "Bloody Sunday" 1972, 1
unarmed Derry people were sho
dead by British soldiers. The wal
allow no one to forget. In front o
a slogan recalling that Sunda
children of the Creggan estate
Derry play at war. The supermarke
trolley serves sometimes as a
armoured vehicle, sometimes a
a prison

VINCENT MENTZ

RENATE VON FORSTER

It was well past midnight at the Golden Pheasant pub in Lisnarrick, County Fermanagh. The music had stopped but the Rock 'n' Rollers hung on. In territory more often associated with marching bands, traditional music and country and western, they live their fantasies in New Jersey and Tennessee. Earlier in the month, Elvis Presley fans had met in commemoration of his death. And in June, over 65,000 people attended Bruce Springsteen's largest-ever concert (at that time) in the grounds of Slane Castle, in County Meath. But rock music is indigenous too. There are soul bands in Sligo, funk bands in Donegal, reggae bands in Limerick and new wave bands in Waterford.

Preceding pages:

Dedaux and Irene McLean of Camarilo, California (left), saw a lot of castles on their tour of Ireland with Halbert's Inc. Heritage Travel of Ohio. At Bunratty Castle, County Clare, just a few miles from Shannon Airport — point of arrival and departure for most of the visting Americans — visitors celebrate their rootedness in old Ireland with a banquet. The Harris sisters (right) came from Holland to join Courtney's, one of the smaller of Ireland's half-dozen circuses which criss-crossed the country through the summer. The last days of August found the gymnast sisters in Knock, a small town and place of pilgrimage in the "snipe country" of east County Mayo.

Following pages:

In 1967, there were 12,681 independent grocers in Ireland. By 1985, almost half of those had gone out of business in the face of the expansion of supermarkets. A mixture of native hustling talent and American marketing techniques has allowed Irish supermarket chains like Superquinn and Dunne's stores to more than hold their own against the British-owned Quinnsworth and Tesco chains. Superquinn, owned by the Dundalk-born Feargal Quinn, was able to invest £9 million in its new Blackrock complex (top left and bottom right), opened in 1985.
Crazy Prices (top right) is part of the Quinnsworth group, Superquinn's biggest competitor. Quinnsworth is in turn part of the Associated British Foods empire, which has an annual profit of over £150 million sterling.

GERAY SWEENEY

MARTIN PARR

On Grafton Street, the beautiful
people parade and the punks hang
out. Dublin's most intensive
commercial area includes the most
expensive boutiques, the fashionable
department stores, as well as a
McDonald's restaurant and a record
shop specialising in the newest new
wave.

At a time when property
development elsewhere in the city
slowed up, Grafton Street and its
immediate vicinity continued to
attract investment – in the Westbury
Hotel and its shopping mall, in the
Powerscourt Townhouse Centre, and,
most recently, in a shopping arcade
being built where once the Royal
Hibernian Hotel stood.
There are also plans for a massive
shops, pubs, and cinema
development on the corner of St.
Stephen's Green, beside the top end
of Grafton Street. This is where the
break-dancers gather, where bible
groups issue their warnings and
where the Hare Krishna chanters ran
into conflict with the garda in August.
A shop owner in Grafton Street gave
away too much in the court case
against one of the Hare Krishna
followers. Grafton Street had been
pedestrianised for the traders, he
said.

Preceding pages:

At about 5.30 p.m. on Sunday, 25th
August, as the free open air concert,
Lark By The Lee in Cork, was
beginning to wind down, Ireland's
most successful rock band, U2,
suddenly appeared before the 7,000-
strong crowd. The concert organisers
from the pop station, RTE Radio 2,
and senior garda officers had kept
the band's appearance secret for
fear of a riot.
U2's last appearance in Ireland had
been in June before a crowd of
65,000 in Croke Park football stadium
in Dublin following a phenomenally
successful tour of the United States.
For that tour they had a p.a. rig
reckoned to be one of the two or
three largest in the world. For their
75-minute show in Cork – from where
most of U2's technical crew come –
they worked with equipment at one
tenth of the capacity. The excitement
was no less great.
At one point during their set, lead
singer Bono asked for an anti-
apartheid banner being held up in the
crowd to be passed up to the stage.
In a rare political gesture – unless a
well-publicised meeting with the
Taoiseach (prime minister) Garret
FitzGerald, counts as such – he held
the banner aloft. Weeks later, Bono
asked a group of anti-apartheid
strikers from Dunne's Stores in Dublin
to join the recording of his
contribution to the **Sun City** album.

At the Whiskey Corner in Ir
Distillers' Dublin headquarters (abo
they serve just one drink – seven, t
or twelve years old. The tradition
style bar, where Whiskey Corr
manager John Ryan welcom
20,000 visitors annually, is part c
museum with bottles, barrels, shov
and stills from the several distiller
which Irish Distillers H
amalgamated to form one of t
country's ten largest priva
companies. The group's seve
different brands are blend
differently, the distilling concentrat
in Dublin, Middleton, County Co
and Bushmills, County Antri
Comedian Hal Roach (below) is o
of the star attractions of Jurys Ir
Cabaret which plays at Jurys Dub
hotel nightly from May to Octob
and also undertakes tours of t
United State

His repertoire of jokes includes t
following: "A little old lady at Dub
Airport flying in from Lourdes w
asked by the customs officer wh
was in the bottle she was carryir
'Oh, officer, 'tis only a drop of hc
water from Lourdes,' she said. Tl
officer took the bottle, opened
tasted the water, and said 'Madar
this is whiskey'. The old lady sai
'Glory be to God . . . a miracle'

Following page

The traditional crafts fac
insuperable odds. The last of tl
Dublin coopers were laid off in 19
and the 300-year-old Regular Dub
Coopers Society was wound u
There are only about 100 full-tin
blacksmiths in the count
The cooper at Bushmills Distille
in north Antrim (left) makes oak va
in which the whiskey matures for
long as 12 years. Bushmills is tl
oldest distillery in the world, datir
back to 1608. The small town on tl
river Bush derived its name from tl
several mills it once had, makir
paper, flour and farm tools ar
dressing flax for the Nortl
traditional linen industr
John Reilly of Dunboyne, Cour
Meath (right), represents the sever
generation of his family in tl
blacksmith's trade. His home, Forg
House, has been a blacksmitl
premises for 200 yea
Mr Reilly's business comes fro
the stud farms in County Mea
and County Kildare and north Coun
Dublin. He shoes up to 30 hors
daily, also making frequent trips
England's stud farm district arour
the Newmarket race cours

TOM KELLY

For Ireland, Love or Money

In the course of the past half century the Irish people have found themselves to be materialists, just like everybody else; and the discovery appears to have occasioned them some surprise. The distance they have travelled in self-awareness can be measured simply. In 1933, Éamon De Valera, then at the beginning of the sixteen unbroken years as head of government which is still, incidentally, a record for a democratically elected European statesman, came to the microphone to express his hopes for the future. Since "Dev" was, among other things, a tenaciously practical politician, what he said is, at this distance of time, quite astonishing.

"The Irish genius," he declared, "has always stressed spiritual and intellectual rather than material values. That is the characteristic that fits the Irish people in a special manner for the task, now a vital one, of helping to save Western civilisation. The great material progress of recent time, coming in a world where false philosophies already reigned, has distorted men's sense of proportion; the material has usurped the sovereignty that is the right of the spiritual. Everywhere today the consequences of this perversion of the natural order are to be seen. Spirit and mind have ceased to rule. The riches which the world sought, and to which it sacrificed all else, have become a curse by their very abundance. In this day, if Ireland is faithful to her mission and, please God she will be, if as of old she recalls men to forgotten truths . . . then, indeed she can do the world a service as great as that which she rendered in the time of Columcille and Columbanus, because the need of our time is in no ways less."

A large part of his audience, we may suppose, listened with enthusiasm — after all, they were to accord him that sixteen years; and in any case this was the stuff on which they had been brought up. It was in all the school books. It was preached from every pulpit. It was enunciated in insidiously genteel tones by the nuns of several rival teaching orders. It was beaten into unwilling listeners by Christian Brothers armed with a leather thong or strap. It was echoed in newspaper editorials on days of national celebration.

But it was not true. The Irish were, by comparison with some others, poor. They were pious, even devout. They were, to a degree, fatalistic, having learned not to yearn for surfeits which were not within reach. But they were no less materially minded than anybody else, as closer examination of certain classes would have shown. And the legend "do chum glóire Dé agus onóra na hÉireann" — for the glory of God and the honour of Ireland — which embellished the schoolbooks did not reflect their attitude to personal advancement either. The advancements open to most in 1933 were not spectacular, a permanent and pensionable post in the middle brackets of the public service being the best that was on offer for large numbers. But what possibilities there were they seized, and it was not for the glory of God or the honour of Ireland that they did so.

Yet the myth lasted for quite a while after Dev's speech; in fact did not begin to fade until the somewhat illusory prosperity of the 1960s brought the heady delights of the western world within many people's reach. Then the Irish took to the most boring forms of consumerism with the same avidity as everyone else. Advertisers began to portray a paradise in which the main problem was to choose between several brands of vodka, makes of motor car, types of continental holiday and sizes of television set. Among the richer elements, now somewhat richer, an older pattern of conspicuous piety and decorous comfort began to give way to a newer one of conspicuous expenditure and indecorous vulgarity. The attainment of a Mercedes Benz for him and a Fiat for her became the dream of the new suburbia.

And, in spite of a decline in comparative living standards, so it has basically remained. The roads into Dublin are choked every day with commuting motor cars. The approaches to country towns have something of the nowhere look of the approaches to towns in the American west.

The video, the hi-fi, the wall to wall carpet, the booze-up in Marbella are now well established as necessities of life. Strangely, those one might expect to be the spokespersons of an alternative way have remained silent. Though the politicians were once loud in their endorsements of the claim that spiritual sustenance was all the Irish looked for, the descent into consumerist tawdriness has not dismayed them. True, Garret Fitzgerald and Richie Ryan have once or twice condemned materialism, but an examination of the small print reveals that they were merely concerned that those lower down the scale should moderate their wage demands. Perhaps more surprisingly the Catholic Church has accepted the inroads of the contemporary international ethos with apparent equanimity. While its stance about legislative matters such as divorce and contraception remains as stubborn as ever, no pastor has gone rampaging among the night-clubs of Leeson Street, where the executive class disports itself, as his predecessors rampaged the hedges to drive out the poor half-hearted hedonists of another day. And even the patrons of the roadhouse hotel discos which have supplanted the ballrooms of romance in country areas have been accommodated by allowing them to attend mass on Saturday evening instead of Sunday morning.

Some of this is no doubt an advance, at least in honesty, as well as from other points of view. Yet it seems odd that materialism and its attendant evils should have been denounced so often when it was thought necessary to keep people content in their poverty, but that the denunciations should have dried up so completely when the Keynesian discovery that it suited the economic system to have them turn unthinking consumers got through. Nor is the thought of the Irish as entirely bereft of any values of their own really an inspiriting one.

Neither the traveller nor the observer of the scene is, however, likely to conclude that this is the case yet. There is a counter-culture, or rather an amalgam of counter-cultures, ranging from political radicalism to a literary tradition of dissent. Though nearly all the strands in this, with the possible exceptions of the Irish language movement and the folk music revival, have been denounced in the past by the guardians of a chaste and incorruptible Irishness as the products of foreign degeneracy it could turn out in the end – to adapt A. E. Housman's phrase – to be a matter of "what God abandoned, these defended".

Besides, the Irish were asked for a long time to live largely on a diet of absolutes, fed to them from many agencies, in the Calvinist north-east as well as in the rest of the country. Though they may have seemed as materially minded as anybody else in recent years, absolutes leave their mark; indeed they sometimes prove an effective training in both scepticism and idealism.

It may be that the problem for the Irish as for others as the crisis of the west deepens will be mere survival. In Ireland, as elsewhere, there will be increasing unemployment, aggravated by the fact that Ireland has an expanding population which is already the youngest in Europe. If capitalism proves flexible enough to provide sufficient palliatives for the unemployed human condition, whether on the level of video nasties or more up market, acceptance and apathy may prove stronger than anything else, but in Ireland's case one somehow doubts it. Even in a world where positive scepticism, idealism, a sense of history as a record of exploitation and the urge to make sense of the human condition were rare, there would remain the question of what survival was for. In Ireland these things are not rare and so the purveyors of a factitious contentment may well have a difficult task ahead of them there.

Raftery, the blind Gaelic poet born in Kiltimagh, County Mayo, 200 years ago, is commemorated in his native place by a lounge in a pub, The Raftery Room, in what claims to have been, in 1958, 'the first pub in Ireland with live music'. The Raftery Room was opened as an extension to the pub in 1960, making a feature of 'talent from the floor'. Raftery had publicly declaimed his verses bemoaning the death of the Gaelic order. A relic of that order is in the 'Celtic' designs on the dancing costume of Sheila Callaghan, 6, who had by August 1985 won ten trophies, one cup and 46 medals and often taken part in the 'talent from the floor'. She stands before the admiring gazes of publican Jerry Walsh who calls up the talent seven nights a week during the summer, and of the County Roscommon band, The Lancers.

Preceding page:

In a seam just deep enough for a man to reach into lying on his side, in a few inches of water, in dark, dust and noise, a lone miner tackles the coal-face at Arigna Collieries in north County Roscommon. The shafts are driven into the side of a hill to extract 1000 tons of bituminous coal a week, mainly for a power station down the hill on the shore of Lough Allen, but also for local schools, hospitals and factories.
Abandoned pit-heads litter the bare hill. Some smaller companies mine the coal deposit, too, but Arigna Collieries, run by the Layden family for a century, is, with just over 200 employees, by far the largest coal mine in operation in Ireland. The mineworkers' disputes with the Leydens have often been long and bitter. Major strikes in 1934, 1969, 1974 and 1978 went on for over two months each. The conditions remain harsh – and the miners paradoxically dependent on the mine owners. Michael Earley, seen here at the coal-face where he has only the occasional company of a helper to remove the coal, wears no mask to protect himself from the dust and, as with other miners, no ear mitts to protect himself against the noise.
In his colourful guise as Michael Earley Muhamad, The Mountain Mauler, he has on occasion fought unofficial "boxing showdowns" with other "Golden Boys of Boxing in the West". One widely advertised fight, with the promised presence of several well-known show business personalities and from which the proceeds were to go to "a worthy cause", never, in fact, took place. But the legend of Muhamad and the Mountain lives on.

Since 1950, Comhaltas Ceoltóirí Éireann, the official body for the promotion of Irish traditional music and dance (an organisation regarded with some scepticism by many traditional musicians) has organised the competitive Fleadh Cheoil na Éireann annually. Since the mid 1960s, when popular interest in traditional music intensified dramatically, it has become a major social event and competition for the right to host the fleadh is keen. There is about £3 million worth of business at stake. On this occasion, the fleadh coincided with the bigger, noisier, even more profitable Rose of Tralee festival, just 17 miles away.

Preceding pages:

The August commemoration of the death of Michael Collins, IRA leader in the War of Independence and leader of the Free State (pro-Treaty) forces in the subsequent civil war, recalls one of the most controversial incidents of an event which divided Irish nationalists bitterly. In August 1922, Michael Collins was ambushed by republicans (anti-Treaty) here at Bealnablath, County Cork, and the emerging Free State lost its most forceful and energetic leader.
The commemoration is full of ironies for Fine Gael, the senior government coalition partner, which stages it as a rival to the several republican commemorations of Wolfe Tone at Bodenstown, County Kildare. For a party with a tough law-and-order image firmly opposed to militant republicanism, Michael Collins, who was ruthless in his guerrilla campaign against the British, shooting British agents in front of their families, is at least an ambivalent hero. Yet it was as personal hero that Foreign Affairs minister Peter Barry dwelt on his achievements at a later Michael Collins seminar.
At the Bealnablath commemoration, however, the tone was rather more academic. The address was delivered by Brian Farrell, political scientist and frontman of Irish television's main current affairs programme, *Today Tonight*. His speech dealt with the Republic as a Catholic mirror-image of the Protestant Northern state.
The event still retains some of its character as a gathering of the faithful. The presence of IRA veterans like John L O'Sullivan (extreme left, top left, on following page) is a firm reminder of the party's past. He was a captain in the Third Cork Brigade of the IRA and was active in the civil war. He was also a founder-member of the Blueshirts, a quasi-fascist organisation which merged with other right-wing groups to form Fine Gael. Modern Fine Gael straddles young urban social democrats, for whom the past is best forgotten, and older members of Mr O'Sullivan's heritage.

The Cairn Lodge boxing club
Crumlin Road, in Belfast, boasts th
juvenile champions among its 30 b
in training, among them William Bo
14, winner of the best boxer award
championships held in Cork in A
1985, and Tommy Waite, 13, who w
the second year schoolboy class at
kil

The club has itself won a troph
named after 1950s pop star Fran
Vaughan — as the best boxing club
the North. Trainer Alec McDonald tal
on aspiring boxers from the age
nine — up to

Support for boxing among Belfas
working class meant that for ma
years the city had more boxing clu
than Dublin, a city twice its size. Af
Barry McGuigan won the wo
featherweight title in June 19
Belfast's clubs were "inundated" w
new application

Born and reared in Clones, Cou
Monaghan, just south of the Bord
Barry McGuigan became a Belfa
boxer — and a British citizen — when
came under the management
bookmaker Barney Eastwood, who h
extensive interests in the ci
Belfast people turned out in thousan
to greet McGuigan when he return
from his title win in London. On Frida
23rd August, at a press conference
Belfast, the boxer's fans got th
reward; it was announced that Ba
McGuigan's first title defence would
staged on his "home" ground at t
King's Hall in Belfast. And
September, before a wildly enthusia
crowd, he held the title against t
challenge of Bernard Taylor, from t
United State

Following page

Steady rain nearly ruined the Moh
Agricultural Show in south Coun
Leitrim, but some buying and sellin
was done and the prizes f
champion beasts awarded (top righ
At Drumshambo cattle and shee
mart in the north of the county (le
the prices were down by as much a
one quarter on the averages for th
summer. Farmers were worried at n
having enough winter fodder ar
were selling stock in some pani
driving prices dow
The hay was beyond saving on th
north County Leitrim farm of Franc
McGuire in Ballinamore where h
brought in a baler to make ba
silag

BILL BIGGART

Long and narrow, a Cork post office became a pub in 1842 and was nick-named the Long Valley by British soldiers, after a rifle range at army headquarters in Aldershot, England. Brothers John King, 57, and Charlie King, 55, live together in Mannon Road, work together bagging and selling coal and drink together in the well-tended establishment of Humphrey Moynahan. Mr Moynahan comes from a family of tailors who bought a pub beside their premises in order to expand their business. The craft-proud tailors concealed their involvement in the less noble trade of publican by adopting the nickname rather than giving it their own family name. When war-time conditions pushed up the price of cloth and forced the Moynahans out of the tailoring business, the pub became their sole – and openly admitted – business.

Following pages:

In the "free airport" industrial zone at Shannon, a South African-owned company produces drilling rods in one of the deepest furnaces in the world. Boart Hard Metals, part of the world-wide Anglo-American Corporation which also has a second, larger subsidiary, De Beers, at Shannon, set up here in 1960 as one of the first arrivals in the free zone. Some of its jumbo drill bits are used in prospecting and gas production off the coast of Ireland and in the mining of Europe's largest lead-zinc deposit in County Meath, but over 90% of the production goes abroad; the incentive from the state is to export.

Boart Hard Metals has over 200 employees. These women have to be well protected from the 1000 degrees Centigrade temperatures of the furnace.

Ireland's new industries have widened the work opportunities for women. But in the electronics and healthcare industries, which have been priority targets of the state's development body, female labour is concentrated in relatively unskilled assembly blending and packaging. Women make up one-third of the total work force but less than one-fifth of those in industry.

CHRISTINE HANSCOMB

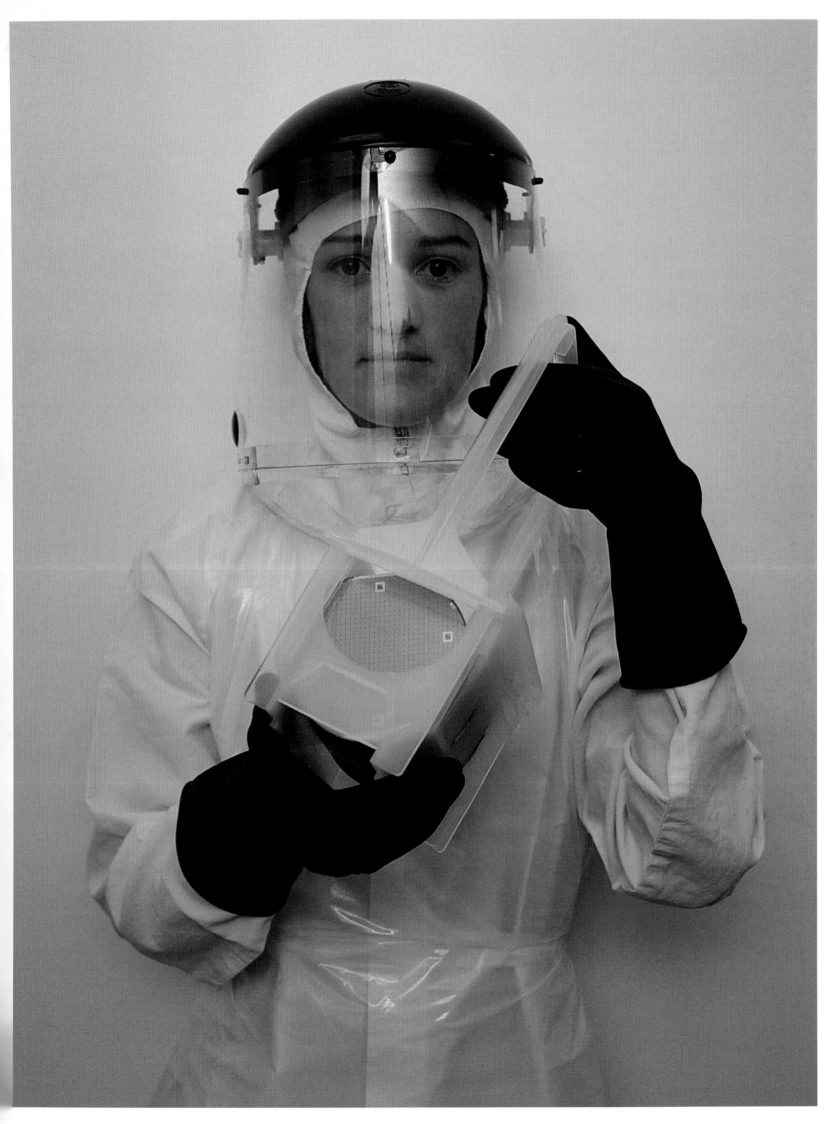

GUGLIELMO GALVIN

The Rose of Tralee contest and the festival around it are an ingenious mixture of patriotism, purity and sex. The beauty contest takes its name and some of its colour from a local anthem which extols not just the beauty in the woman it praises but "the truth in her eyes ever dawning". The contest brings together women of Irish extraction from Australia, North America, New Zealand, Britain and all counties of Ireland in a celebration of the Irish diaspora. Perrine Phipps (following pages, far right) was the 1985 contestant from the British Midlands.

The usual carnality of the beauty contest is restrained by the requirement that the finalists be interviewed by Gay Byrne, Ireland's leading television personality, and that they perform a "party piece". Gay Byrne, now an integral part of the institution, is, according to the opinion polls, the most popular man in Ireland. He has hosted (and produced) the **Late Late Show** since the early 1960s.

His presiding presence and that of local TD (member of Parliament) and Tánaiste (deputy prime minister), Dick Spring (following pages, bottom left, with moustache), who performed the official opening ceremony on 24th August, confer respectability on an occasion of much late-night revelry.

Preceding pages:

At 7 a.m., a team of five filleters begins work at Peter Forman and Sons Ltd, in Howth, a fishing and sailing harbour eight miles out of Dublin.

Cod, whiting, plaice, ray, haddock, monkfish, brill, turbot, herrings, and hake have been bought from the trawlers on the previous evening. The filleters have them ready for distribution to shops and restaurants by mid-morning. This morning Martin Mahony, Nick Loughlin, Patrick Reed and Tom Moore have their knives drawn.

At the **Irish Times** printing press in Dublin city centre, James Dunne, Noel Cooke and Rupert O'Reilly check the first edition of 27th August . The newspaper went through its own rationalisation and modernisation programme following commercial and editorial difficulties in the mid-1970s. A successful editor, Douglas Gageby, left, then returned. The company diversified into retail shops, then sold them off.

Computerised typesetting was introduced in the early 1980s and the former (mainly Protestant) director-shareholders sold their stake. Control passed to a newly appointed trust, charged with preventing a takeover and with safeguarding the paper's identity.

JERRY GORDON

The rapid growth of Dublin's southside suburbs in the 1960s brought new openings for large supermarkets catering for customers with cars. The Dunne family, who wholly own and control a large group of retail stores around the country, were one of the first to realise the opportunity when they opened the Cornelscourt centre.

Ben Dunne, paterfamilias and founder of the group which has become the largest private Irish company, was a devout Catholic who never flaunted his wealth but lived the last years of his life quietly in the exclusive Shelbourne Hotel. He modelled Dunnes Stores as a down-market version of the British retail chain Marks and Spencer, operating with high turnover and low costs (including labour costs), and maintaining both food and drapery branches of the business under one roof.

His son, also Ben Dunne, now runs the business. In 1981 he was kidnapped by the IRA but released, allegedly after the payment of a large ransom.

A Dunne's Stores branch in the centre of Dublin became involved in a long and bitter industrial dispute following the sacking of women workers who refused to handle South African goods in July 1984. On the night of 23/24 August 1985, over a year later, a group of strikers and supporters occupied the shop, timing their exit on the Saturday afternoon to coincide with the expected visit of a representative of the African National Congress.

The management of Dunne's Stores, which is unfriendly to trade unions and actively discourages fraternisation between even junior management and ordinary employees, has remained unbending in the face of pleas from, amongst others, Irish bishops and Bishop Desmond Tutu of South Africa. And the strikers became international celebrities in trade union and progressive political circles.

MARTIN PARR

Pat Coyle (left) and huntsma
Éamonn Coyle cut up the carcass
a cow to feed the hounds of th
Ward Union Hunt in County Meat
The cow went to feed dogs rath
than humans because it had died o
the farm, not in the supervise
conditions of an abattoir or mea
factor

Based just 15 miles outside Dubl
city, the hunt meets regularly in th
winter months to hunt stag which ar
reared in captivity and released fo
the chase but never, in fact, caugh
by the hounds. Deer do breed in th
wild in mountainous and woode
parts of Ireland but they are strictl
protected

TOM KELLY

Phil Munnelly's family band from Crossmolina, County Mayo, plays mostly for dinner dances, cabarets and weddings. Mr Munnelly is the owner of a general hardware and fancy goods store who played professionally in the ballrooms for 15 years until 1964, when he married. In 1980, he formed the family group with his three daughters, Kathy, Sharon and Aundre, plus son Phil. During the summer, they may do five appearances each week, mostly at weddings. In the winter they provide the music for dinner dances, organised by sports clubs, community organisations and commercial enterprises, on two or three nights a week.

Kathy Munnelly, Phil's wife, runs a hairdressing salon and there are two more children in the family, Emer and Irene, who also play musical instruments.

Following pages:

Ireland may have been too poor to develop a coherent tradition of its own vernacular architecture. There was little or nothing between the damp and dark, if now picturesque, rural thatched cottages and the haughty elegance of the Georgian town houses in the city. New houses in the countryside do maintain some sort of continuity with the old cottages by their one-storey layout and simple design, but at the same time try for a more affluent effect and are often placed in the most prominent possible site, like this one (left) on the side of a hill. Latticed windows follow a "Georgian" fashion which is more directly reflected in Dublin suburban houses (right). With the actual destruction of much of Georgian Dublin through the 1960s and 1970s, nostalgia produced a mock-Georgian trend in expensive middle-class housing. Latticed windows and plastic pseudo-classical pillars were worth at least a few thousand pounds on the price of the house, allowing, as they did, some sense of identification for the new rich with the graciousness of the old ascendancy. Red brick, for so long associated with dereliction and decay, has come back into use in Dublin buildings – in part under direction from the planning authorities – as homage to the city's most distinctive architectural period.

Within weeks, Anthony Boyle would no longer enjoy the privilege of being, at 11, the country's youngest exchange operator on his days off school. The switchboard at Burtonport, County Donegal, "went automatic" in September 1985 as the drive intensified to have all of the Republic's phones routed directly through the digital network by 1987. In mid-1985, there were still 20,000 lines in four western counties, including Donegal, which only connected with the outside world when someone at the exchange responded to a cranking handle or a banging receiver.

With the lines by-passing manual exchanges, the principal collators of insignificant and indispensable information were cut off from a prime source. The postmaster or postmistress who plugged in and out, and might not always do either in full haste, was often the first to know of the child born, the cousin returning, or the farm for sale.

In the early hours of Saturday morning, the motor tanker **Anna Borere** heads out of Dublin for Swansea, in Wales. The ship's delivery of the chemical acrylo-nitrile was one of the few freight consignments, other than those arriving by container, to be unloaded at Dublin during the summer. A strike by deep-sea dockers, over terms for their further reduction in numbers to one quarter of 1970 levels, lasted ten weeks. From Dublin, the highly volatile chemical is transported over 170 miles overland to the Japanese-owned Asahi textile spinning works at Killala, County Mayo. Killala has a harbour but it would have needed expensive development to provide berthing facilities for such tankers. So the poisonous chemical is unloaded at Dublin, obliging fire authorities in eight counties to adopt a contingency plan to deal with the emergency which would arise from a spillage.

Following pages:

The port of Derry is a shadow of what it was 15 years ago. Then, there were 20 berths in use; today, that number has fallen to two. All of the 45 dockers are casual workers, signing on at the "bru" (labour exchange) when they are not working.

On the weekend of 24th/25th August a consignment of smokeless fuel brought in from Rotterdam by the Bilbao-registered **Uralar Cuarto** was being unloaded.

Coal had come into Derry port during the British coal-miners' strike, when dockers in Britain were refusing to handle imported coal.

Other imports into Derry are grain, fertilisers and seed potatoes, grown in Cyprus in varieties especially suitable to County Donegal, the traditional commercial potato-growing county. The much more limited exports include scrap metal and pulpwood.

JOHN P. COYLE

There was a large field of
runners for the last race of the day
Phoenix Park Racecourse
Saturday, 24th August (top). This wa
the Rohan Group Two-Year-O
Maiden, for young horses still
score their first win. Mrs Bertra
Firestone, Major Victor McCalmo
and Lady Sarah Barry were amon
the leading horse-owners giving the
unproven horses a ru
People of more mode
circumstances make up a large pa
of the crowd at Phoenix Park, on th
edge of Dublin city. In the gener
enclosure and out along the rai
(below) are those with a £5 or £
stake in the outcome of a rac
In the owners' and trainer
enclosure that day were some of th
country's top businessmen, amon
them Tony O'Reilly, international vice
president of the Heinz Corporation
and chairman of the Independen
Newspapers group, as well as of a
Irish investment company, and an c
exploration firm, and Michael Smurfi
head of Ireland's most successfu
manufacturing company, makers c
paper and packaging materials, a
well as an owner of horses an
sponsor of races
On the day of the race meeting,
became known that independen
Newspapers were bidding along wit
Vernon Pools for the franchise to ru
a proposed new national lottery (the
bid was unsuccessful). Vernon Pools
owner Robert Sangster was also a
"the Park". A major bloodstock owne
Mr Sangster was one of the
consortium which revitalised the old
racecourse, originally built in
Edwardian times and modelled on
London's Hurst Park. The racecourse's
new facilities include a beef bar and a
disco/nightclub

Faiths and Families

In recent years the religiosity of the Irish has become something of a scandal, at least to those who are heirs to the liberal, sceptical traditions of western Europe. There is widely believed to be a religious war in progress there, something which the rest of Europe has not seen since the 17th century. The Catholic Church is known to have enormous political influence in the Republic, the Constitution of which begins with an invocation to the Most Holy Trinity. Every night during the period when the photographs in this book were being taken thousands stood in the rain in a field in Cork, gazing fixedly at a statue of the Blessed Virgin, which some people claimed they had seen move. Every Sunday night in Belfast, fervent, sometimes delirious audiences drink in the fiery doctrines of an unmellowed Calvinism.

And so on and so forth. At least three generations of novelists having portrayed a puritanical society in which male and female virginity was still rife, tyrannical parish priests policed the lanes and frustrated males sought sublimation in the bottle, the accepted picture changed slightly. Ireland, according to the northern poets, was a country where religious bigotry flourished and the religion of one's neighbours was a primary concern.

And some of it is true, or partly true. Religion does play a larger part in the life of Ireland than it does in that of most countries of the western tradition. One has only to watch the crowds streaming out of mass or chapel on a Sunday to see that. There is a good deal of bigotry in the north-east corner and some in all the nine counties of Ulster. During the time in which our photographers were let loose on the land there were moving statues and apparitions everywhere, not just in Cork. The sale of contraceptives has only just become legal in the Republic. The Catholic Church effectively controls education. There is an Irish asceticism, dating back to early Christian times; and an Irish abnegation, product of rural conditions. The churches, Catholic and Presbyterian, have more than their share of power.

But to attribute even the power or popularity of religion to faith alone is to suggest that religion exists in a social vacuum and that people do not accept, or use, religion for social purposes.

In Ireland since the 17th century the various Christian religions have appeared to command extraordinary loyalties and to give rise to fierce passions, while the Catholics at least seemed prepared to endure bitter persecution for the sake of their faith.

But the ethnic, cultural and social cleavages which religious difference paralleled were not caused by it. True, religious conflict aggravated them. Equally, it sometimes masked them. But they had a reality of their own. And, unfortunately, some of them still have.

Britain became a Protestant power just at the time when absolute monarchies were consolidating their grip everywhere in Europe and so the decision to reduce the Catholic nobility of Ireland to subservience had an element of religious persecution in it. It became involved in a life and death strategic struggle in which the lines of division were Catholic and Protestant shortly afterwards; and so the existence of Catholicism in Ireland became a danger. Britain was newly Protestant just at the time when colonisation became a fashionable cure for the Irish problem at the English court. So the colonists were Protestant. So were Cromwell's soldiers when he in his turn decided that he could arrive at a final solution to the Irish question by giving them the country as booty. The struggle between native and planter was therefore imbued with religion from the beginning as was the subsequent landlord-tenant conflict in Ireland. Ethnic and social divisions were exacerbated by religious ones, and had, as we would say nowadays, a religious dimension to them.

And, naturally, religious divisions were in their turn exacerbated and fixed by social gulfs and social considerations. When two separated middle classes emerged in the 19th century they competed for jobs and commercial advantages along religious lines. When an industrial working class emerged from the rural population in the north-east it could be, and was, divided and exploited along religious lines. It is difficult to escape the conclusion that much of what has passed for religious passion in Ireland in the last 150 years was merely a passion for respectability as a proof of social worthiness. If Catholics had the name of being dirty, ignorant and shiftless they would prove that they were otherwise by outdoing Protestants in certain ways, the difference between a stricter morality and a greater respectability not always being apparent, least of all to the parties themselves. And certainly much of what has passed for religious faith and religious loyalty in the last 200 years has been loyalty to something else. A Catholic who abandoned his or her religion was a bad patriot. A Protestant who did likewise was disloyal to the Crown, the British connection and all those who were dependent on it.

So it may be that the Irish have got the name and the glory of being faithful unto death to their religions when it was really something else they were being faithful to, their class or their country or their social group or even their language. And likewise of course got the name of being bigots when they were only pursuing social advantage. As in Poland, religion and nationalism became in Ireland inextricably mixed. So did religion and loyalty to the crown.

And partition established not one sectarian state but two. If Sir James Craig could have "a Protestant Parliament for a Protestant people", so, with somewhat more justification since its population was less mixed, could the rulers of the new Free State. The sort of Catholic triumphalism with which the 26 Counties greeted the end of the eight centuries of British rule would not have been possible if all 32 counties had become independent at the same time; or plausible if sufficient numbers of Protestants had followed the example of Wolfe Tone, Thomas Davis and Charles Stewart Parnell and thrown in their lot with the independence movement. One of the main effects of the Anglo-Irish agreement or "treaty" of 1922, which established the Free State, was to give middle-class Catholics in the 26 Counties more leverage in banking and business, legal and academic circles. It was natural therefore that the ruling group should treat the advent of Irish independence as a splendid victory for Catholicism.

But if all this is, looked at in one way, a tragi-comedy of errors and of labels it has its more cheerful implications for the future. With the ending of certain social dominances or desperations would come an end to the more unsavoury expressions of religious zeal. The 26-county state has, in spite of the theological bias of some of its legislation, a good record where religious equality is concerned. Its stance on contraception and other matters is not an expression of anti-Protestantism; merely of a medievalist dislike of the contemporary world. When certain long-standing historical pressures and antagonisms are eased, everybody will become much more relaxed about religion too.

Kieron James Byrne, born on 25th July, was the first child of John Byrne and Catherine Farrington. At five weeks, he was christened at St Columba's Church in Glasnevin, north Dublin. The godparents were Mr Byrne's brother, James, and Celine Kenny. Monsignor Tom Fehily performed the ceremony.

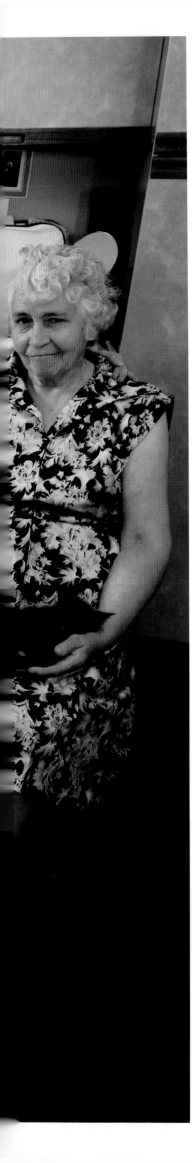

George Mernagh built the four-bedroom bungalow near Tullow, County Carlow, where he and his wife Johanna live with their three children, Susan, 12, Fergus, 9, and Kenneth, 4, Mrs Mernagh's widowed mother, Ester Byrne, Lassie, the dog, and a cat.

Mr Mernagh is a building contractor, constructing individual houses and bungalows, together with his single employee. He used to employ more workers but in 1985 building had "gone slack".

Mrs Mernagh is a member of the Ballyconnell guild of the Irish Countrywomen's Association. Susan enjoys Irish dancing. Fergus is a keen runner.

Following pages:

The Gentlemen's Bathing Place at Sandycove, County Dublin, has been a gentlemen-only spot for many decades — and remains so despite a well publicised raid on it by a group of women activists.

There are many daily all-year-round bathers at the Forty Foot, as it is known, braving not only the cold — including the cold of Monday, 26th August — but also the rising levels of pollution in Dublin Bay.

Messages of hope and salvation are displayed by Protestant churches, fundamentalist and gospel groups on gable walls, hay barns and advertising hoardings. This one is on the road between the seaside towns of Portrush and Portstewart. In Portrush, on Sunday, 26th August, there was a gospel meeting in a tent on the beach; in Portstewart, another on the sea-front.

A vast variety of Protestant groups and churches, many with lay preachers, meet in modest churches and primitive halls throughout the North.

KEVIN O'FARRELL

Michael Mullen, 46, and Julia Faherty 28, joined about 30 guests at their wedding reception in Gilbert's Guest House on Inishmore, largest of the Aran Islands. Theirs was one of the half-dozen weddings celebrated on the islands in 1985. For over 20 years, the islanders have preferred to get married in Galway on the mainland where hotels are geared — as one of their most profitable activities — to providing chicken-and-ham meals to large numbers of guests. Away from the islands, the families involved can also control the number of guests — and their budgets — more easily. This party in the guest house was modest enough. Afterwards, the whole population of the island, it seemed, joined in the festivities.

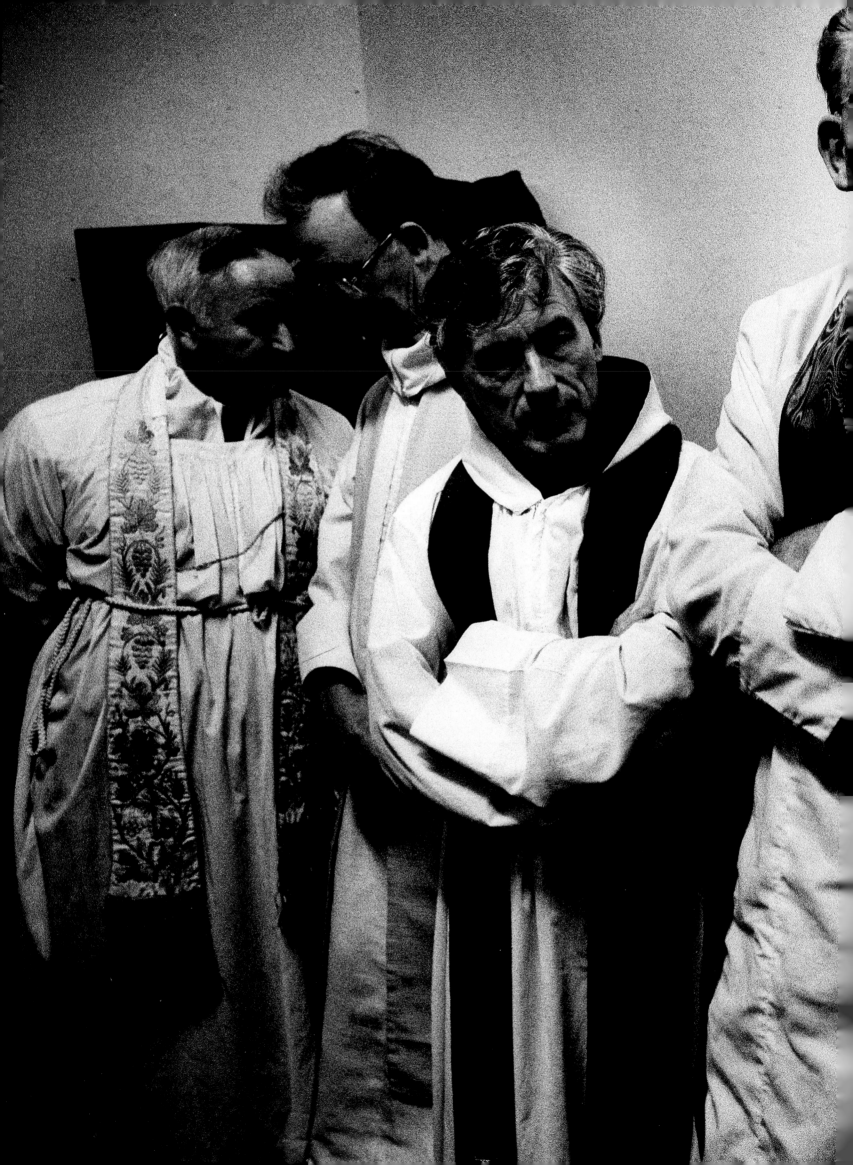

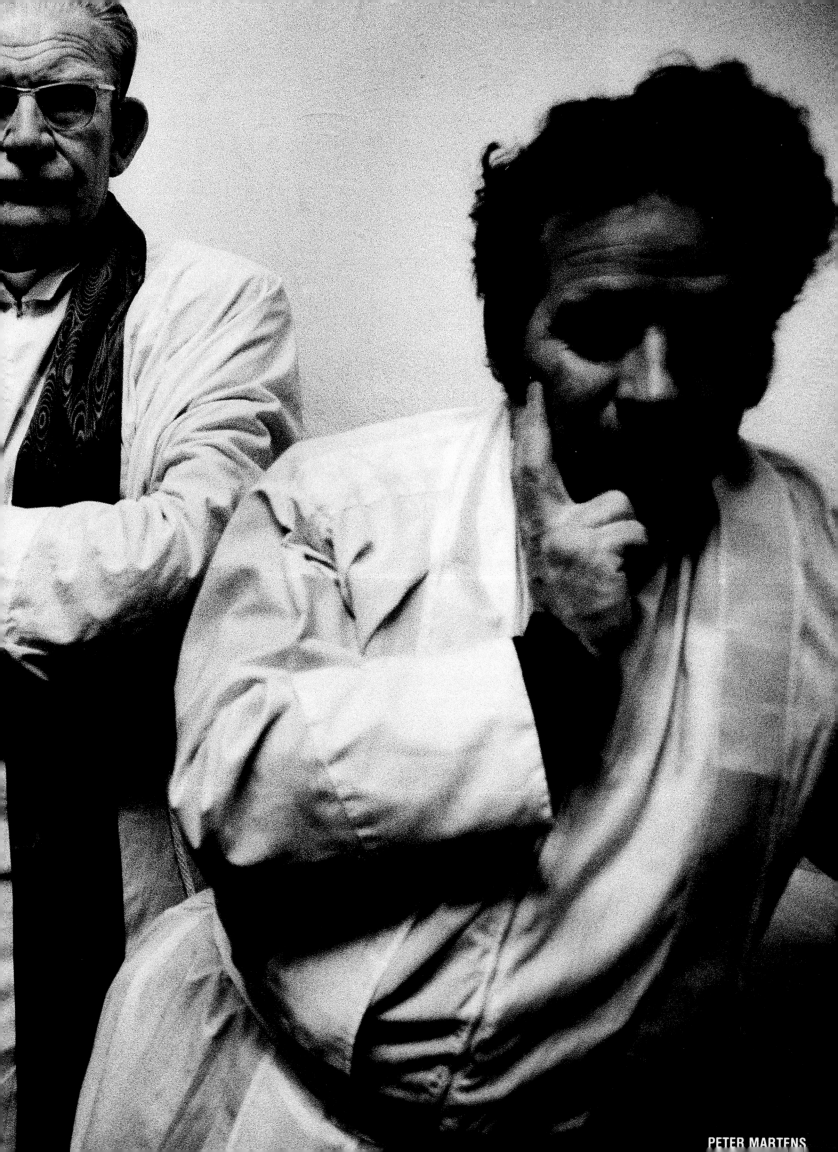

The comfort given to the families who came with their mentally or physically handicapped children, brothers or sisters to a special mass in Carrickmore, County Tyrone, could be plainly felt as they all relaxed later with some entertainment and with tea and buns.

Four local priests said the mass in a community hall in the strongly nationalist town on the afternoon of Saturday, 24th August. The handicapped, many of them seriously disabled would not usually be brought to church on a Sunday.

Preceding page:

The 70 Cistercian monks at Mount Melleray had begun their observances at 3.45 a.m. with the Vigil. They returned then to their room, re-assembling for the Eucharist at 5.10, then read in silence until the Morning Lauds at 8 a.m.

Only then did they speak to each other, having maintained their silence for the 12 hours since their bed-time the previous night. Only if there is an urgent matter to be dealt with, do they communicate and then only by sign language.

The monks are seen here just before High Mass, con-celebrated at noon by a group of monks with a congregation of local people. Visitors have always been welcome at Mount Melleray since the Cistercians established their house there, in the Knockmealdown mountains of west County Waterford, in 1833.

Daniel O'Connell, nationalist leader and champion of Catholic Emancipation, was one of the early guests. Éamon de Valera, late President of Ireland, was a regular visitor up to the last days of his life.

Alcoholics, poets, philosophers have all come here in search of quiet and solitude. All observe the regime of self-suffiency and silence, which up to recent years was even more rigorous.

Guests are not asked to pay; the monks maintain their community by growing the ingredients of their vegetarian diet, and selling the production of their 200-strong dairy herd and their poultry farm. But from time to time, they have also had to sell some of the contents of their rich library to raise funds.

The Cistercians came to Ireland in 1142 and built a number of the most striking ecclesiastical buildings in the country, among them Jerpoint Abbey and Duiske Abbey in County Kilkenny, Mellifont Abbey in County Louth, and Boyle Abbey in County Roscommon, all of them beautifully situated in verdant valleys.

First day at boarding school for (left to right) David Flanagan, from County Laois, Bryan Hanrahan, from County Kilkenny, Fergus Keane, from County Cork, and Charles Keane, from County Cork. Their families, from the wealthy farmers and provincial professionals, will pay over £2000 per annum to have the boys educated at Rockwell College by the Holy Ghost Fathers.

The college is on a large property in County Tipperary, with an extensive farm, a forest, a lake and plentiful playing fields. Its fees put it among the ten most expensive schools in the Republic.

The President of Ireland, the Attorney General, an Irish rugby international, a champion jockey and members of parliament of both major parties in the Republic are among the past pupils. The late president Éamon de Valera taught here, having been a student – as was Bob Geldof much later – at the sister college in Blackrock, Co. Dublin. Novelist Liam O'Flaherty, poet Pádraic Ó Conaire and Cardinal Michael Browne were Rockwell students.

Rockwell has 400 pupils in its secondary school, another 110 students at its agricultural college and a further 125 on a three-year course at a catering college. In November 1985, the college was cited by former Taoiseach, Jack Lynch, as one of the religious-run colleges where Gaelic games were "effectively" banned. College president Father Michael Hurley insisted that Gaelic football and hurling were encouraged at Rockwell – alongside rugby, canoeing and horse riding. These first-day 12-year-olds came complete with their golf clubs.

Following pages:

On Sherkin Island, off the coast of south-west County Cork, Mairead and Geraldine Clifford are on holiday from their home in north county Kerry and Ronan and Eoghan Collins pass the time out of the local primary school, which has just 18 pupils. At one time, the school population sank to three but the total numbers on the island have risen steadily over the past decade to more than 100. More of the young people from the families of fishermen and farmers are staying rather than emigrating. And there has been an influx of new inhabitants – from England, Denmark, the Netherlands and the United States – in search of a simple, fulfilling life. On Sherkin, as on other coastal islands, the population has become more vocal in demanding better facilities – basic things like ferries and phones. They have also set up their own co-operatives to provide services independently and to give some employment in manufacturing.

PETER LAVERY

MARKETA LUSKACOVA

On Sunday morning, 25th August, over 500 people packed into St Eugene's parish hall in Derry's Bogside area to hear two American Jesuit priests, brothers Des Linn and Matthew Linn, explain and demonstrate the power of healing in prayer and in the sacraments. At one point, those in the crowd were asked to play the part of Jesus to the person beside them, allowing the healing power to pass through them. Then the roles of each pair were reversed.

Nearly one half of those present had said they were suffering from some disorder or another. Asked later if they felt relief, some who had earlier said they were suffering had answered "yes".

The event was organised by the Derry Renewal Group, one of the lay groups of "charismatic" inspiration which have sprung up in recent years in the Irish Catholic Church, tolerated and even encouraged by individual priests, but still marginal to the body of the Church as a whole.

American "healing priests" have found a ready and numerous following in Ireland. A week later, Father Joe Maguire, from Boston, preached to crowds of several thousand a time at Dublin churches. He said he had received 15,000 letters from Ireland, after his last visit, asking him to return.

At another series of highly charged rallies in October, the American Redemptorist priest, Father Ed McDonough, also visiting Dublin, was said to have helped disabled people walk and partially sighted people to see better.

Preceding pages:

The funeral of Daniel Mallon took place at the Sacred Heart Church in Strabane, County Tyrone, on Saturday, 24th August. Mr Mallon, a 65-year-old Catholic, and retired shopkeeper, was shot two days earlier in a local pub when two IRA men came in, called out the name of a Protestant friend of his, and he turned around.

The IRA later admitted its mistake, expressing its "deep regret". Their intended victim was a contractor who worked on the repair and maintenance of police barracks. On the previous day, at Coalisland, County Tyrone, Seamus McAvoy, a Catholic business man was buried. He, too, did contract work for the Royal Ulster Constabulary and was shot by the IRA at his home in Dublin. Politicians and priests claimed he had been the target of extortion bids.

MARKETA LUSKACOVÁ

A small number of religious zealots maintain a very visible and vociferous presence on Dublin's streets, parading outside the Dáil (parliament) building, warning of the dire consequences of extending the sale of contraceptives or legislating for divorce, or protesting over Dublin Corporation's removal of a Marian statue erected illegally on a pedestrian island in the main street.

Following pages:

The Franciscan Sisters of St Mary have a universal mission, with members spread through 71 countries. This retired nun (top right) has returned after many years' work in Nigeria to the order's house at Lough Glynn, near Castlerea, County Roscommon, where the sisters' mission is to care for the elderly. Earlier in August, the Mother-General of the world-wide order also returned to Lough Glynn, to her own birth-place and to the convent at which she had entered the order in 1947. Sister Maura O'Connor spent most of her years as a missionary in India and became head of an order with over 9,000 members in 1984. Many Irish missionaries and former missionaries to the Third World have in recent years abandoned their traditional quietism at home to practise liberation theology's "option for the poor" in Ireland. Some played a central part in the opposition to President Reagan's visit to Ireland in 1984, condemning, in particular, his government's role in Central America and the Philippines where Irish missionaries are active. Some have identified the travellers as a kind of Third World within Ireland. At Foxford, County Mayo, the Irish Sisters of Charity, with a community of 15, and a convent school, have been making rugs, blankets, tweeds and furnishing fabrics since 1892 (bottom left). Providence Woollen Mills was set up to provide local employment in a district which had, and still has, no other major source of employment. Eighty-year-old looms, which once were powered by the river Moy, along with more modern machinery produce £2 million worth of goods annually. Sisters Ronan and Colette, both from Dublin (bottom left), are among the nuns who look after the company's administration and financial management.

RENATE VON FORSTER

PIERRE TOUTAIN

In the past few years there has been a slight but steady increase in the number of registry office weddings in Ireland; the numbers, however, remain tiny. More and more couples are taking the option of a wedding in Rome, combining a holiday in the sun, with a pilgrimage to the capital of Catholicism and, more importantly, avoiding the task of feeding hordes of friends and relations. But even as the bills for ordinary weddings mount into the thousands of pounds, the white family wedding remains overwhelmingly popular.

The business has become more organised. Hotels now advertise their wedding facilities on the radio, small country hotels host annual "wedding fairs" where companies display their dresses, jewellery and services, and chic wedding boutiques such as the Pro-Nuptia chain have opened in Dublin and elsewhere.

In a country where there is still no divorce, the financial burden of the public enactment of the wedding in front of the extended family and dozens of friends usually falls on the bride's father. But the act is also a guarantee of the seriousness and permanence of the arrangement. This wedding, in the Banna Beach Hotel, Ardfert, County Kerry, joined together Michael Grady and Martina Connolly, both from Ballyduff.

Preceeding pages:

Incense wafting in mists around the coffin; good wood to be buried in; holy water splashed in blessing before the box is carried from the church; the dim fire of flickering candles to light the way; the dull thud of the earth on the lid. The traditional Catholic rites of death emphasised the natural elements, giving security and continuity through the natural substances. And the grieving Virgin shared the burden of mourning the loss.

The rites have change. The undertakers have become morticians, most of the dead in the cities now wait to be buried, not in their homes but in American-style funeral parlours. Wreaths encased in plastic cover the graves. When the coffin is lowered, the open grave is covered with a green synthetic sheet, made to look like grass, and the soil, filled in later, when the mourners have gone.

The small statue of the Blessed Virgin Mary on a grave in a County Kerry graveyard (left) is of the kind bought in Lourdes or Knock. The plastic containers of flowers (right) are on the adjacent graves of two brothers-in-law, who died within weeks of each other in Carrickmore, County Tyrone.

JERRY GORDON

ALEN MACWEENEY

The men stay at the back duri
mass in St. Patrick's churc
Crossmaglen. The native parish
the head of the Catholic church
Ireland, Cardinal Tomás Ó Fiaic
extends, like the cardina
archdiocese of Armagh, across t
Border. The three churches of t
parish – Crossmagle
Glassdrummond and Shelagh – a
under the care of Canon O'Ne
The men are virtually on their ov
as Saturday night drinking gets unc
way in the sombre but friendly Tels
pub in Derry's Creggan district. T
windows are boarded up, t
curtains drawn, there was
entertainment, apart from televisi
and darts. The place was forbiddir
but the patrons were hospitable a
delighted to welcome t
photographer
"I'm a republican, if you do
mind," said one as he raised I
glass to the came

Preceding pag

The island wedding over, the dress
are washed before being put awa
From the wardrobe, Máirín Connea
on Inishmaan, second largest of t
Aran Islands, has taken a shawl whi
has become a rare treasure. She liv
alone in Cregg village in a traditior
cottage, where the family portrait
photograph of the Galway Bay saili
boat, the hooker, and the Sacr
Heart are prominently displaye
There is also a television, cover
with a cloth when not in use. M
Conneally can plug into the world
Dallas, Dynasty and **Miami Vic**
She speaks no English. There is
average two hours of programmes
Irish every week on Irish televisic
Máirín Conneally was born in t
years immediately after the regu
summer visits to the Aran islands
the playwright John Millington Syng
who developed the plot of TI
Playboy of the Western World fro
stories he heard here. The play h
become an international class
representing the people of the We
in what Synge described in his bo
The Aran Islands, as their "stran
simplicit
Synge also noted that "the wom
are the great conservative force
this matter of the language". T
television in Máirín Conneall
cottage, and in many more, mak
the conservation ever more diffic

MIKE ABRAHAMS △   MARKETA LUSKACOVA

PETER MARTENS

Herding the cows up and down the narrow leafy lanes of County Monaghan, Caroline O'Neill, 5, plays her part – as do her three brothers and sisters – in the running of the family farm. Seán and Mary O'Neill have a herd of 27 cows – about average size for the country's 80,000 dairy farms, but more than the average among the small holdings of County Monaghan where the O'Neills live close to the Border at Scotstown. The children help in the evenings and in their holidays from school, taking the cows to and from the milking parlour, where Mrs O'Neill generally looks after the milking, before seeing to the family's feeding. The milk goes to Ballinode creamery about three miles away, and from there to Monaghan Co-operative, which owns Ballinode and many more of the formerly independent local creameries dotted around the county.

Like many more farming families, the O'Neills have to cope with the problems of a scattered property, living in a house some distance from where they keep their stock on land formerly farmed by Mr O'Neill's parents, who continue to live in the farmhouse attached to that land.

Preceding pages:

A small Marian grotto beside the small village of Ballinspittle in County Cork had become a major resort and place of pilgrimage by August 1985, two months after a group of local people reported having seen the 30-year-old statue move. Within days, the crowds of worshippers there had built up to several thousand each night. And over the following weeks, statues of the Virgin Mary and of Christ crucified at 30 places around the country were said to have been moving, speaking or showing apparitions.

Coach firms organised trips to Ballinspittle, and, as the car registration numbers indicate, families drove over 350 miles from County Sligo to the shrine. Most visitors during July, August and September said they had seen some movement of the hands or face of the statue which is lit indirectly and stands some 15 metres away from the roadside.

By October the crowds had dwindled to a handful and statues elsewhere had become stationary again.

JOAN RUSSELL

JAKE WALLIS

MARKETA LUSKACOVA   BILL KIRK

BUZZ LOGAN
CHARLES TRAUB
JEREMY NICHOLL

SANDI HABER

GERAY SWEENEY   VINCENT MENTZEL

MIKE ABRAHAMS

DENIS WAUGH

RENATE VON FORSTER

EDDIE KULIGOWSKI

FRANK MILLER

TOM KELLY

FERGUS BOURKE
GUGLIELMO GALVIN
PIERRE TOUTAIN   TONY O'SHEA
MARTIN PARR
RED SAUNDERS
JULIEN J   BILLY STICKLAND

ALEN MACWEENEY

PETER LAVERY

DAVID HURN   BARRIE ROKEACH
BILL OWENS

JERRY GORDON   PETER MARTENS

JOHN CLARIDGE

DEREK SPEIRS
CHRISTINE HANSCOMB
SYD SHELTON

SUE PACKER

Photographers

MIKE ABRAHAMS   LONDON, ENGLAND

FERGUS BOURKE   DUBLIN, IRELAN

JOHN CLARIDGE   LONDON, ENGLAND

GUGLIELMO GALVIN   LONDON, ENGLAND

JERRY GORDON   NEW YORK, USA

SANDI HABER   NEW YORK, USA

CHRISTINE HANSCOMB   LONDON, ENGLAND

DAVID HURN   GWENT, WALES

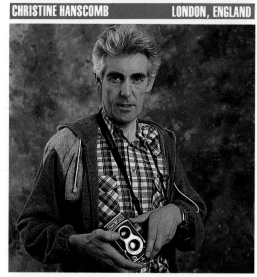

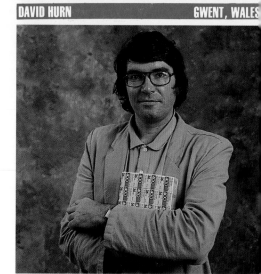

TOM KELLY   COUNTY MEATH, IRELAND

BILL KIRK   BELFAST, IRELAND

EDDIE KULIGOWSKI   PARIS, FRANC

KE ABRAHAMS

nder member of the
ndon-based Network
ture agency, his work
ublished regularly in
nday Times Magazine
d Observer Magazine,
well as in a wide range
British and international
blications. Born in
52, he was brought up
Liverpool, England, and
died photography at
Polytechnic of Central
ndon. He has been a
l-time freelance since
75 working primarily as
ocumentary
otographer.

rahams uses a Leica
2 and Nikon FM and FE.
e Leica basically for
W. Lens: 28mm,
mm, and 50mm. Nikon
colour, lens 24mm
d 35mm.
ght: Flash: Sunpak.
nd held, no tripods.
m: B&W – 400ASA
ed normal, processed
aight.
lour: Kodachrome 64.

ges:
. 59. 62-63. 200-201.
3.

ANDI HABER

ew York-based freelance
otographer, whose
rk in recent years has
peared in magazines
ch as *Esquire,*
ademoiselle and
anhattan. Born in
ennsylvania, in 1956 she
udied photography at
e Rochester Institute of
chnology in New York
ate and psychology in
. She has
rticipated in group
hibitions seen through-
t the United States, and
nce 1980 has had solo
ows in Rochester, San
ancisco, Los Angeles,
cson and Sante Fe. Her
rk is also included in
e collections of
useums in New York,
icago and Los Angeles.

aber works on a
ecially adapted 120
mera creating a
ontage in camera
ns: 80mm
ght: Natural light, hand
ld
m: Vericolor S or L
20

ges:
4-165

FERGUS BOURKE

A photographer for over
25 years, his work has
been exhibited in 14 solo
shows since 1961 when
he exhibited photographs
of Dublin street scenes.
His work has been
published in a wide range
of international
magazines, among them
Modern Photography,
Vogue, Time, Observer
Magazine, and *New York*
Times Magazine. He has
been a member of the
Irish artists' assembly,
Aosdana, since its
inception in 1982.

Bourke uses Mamiya twin
lens reflex and shoots
only in B&W.
Lens: 80mm.
Light: available light in a
daylight studio at the
bottom of his garden;
overhead skylight,
window behind his back
and reflectors. Camera on
tripod.
Film: 400ASA rated
normal, processed
straight.

pages:
136-137.

CHRISTINE HANSCOMB

A full-time photographer
since 1978, she was born
in 1946, graduated in
graphic design in the late
1960s and worked for ten
years as art editor with
Vogue and *Brides*
magazines in London. As
a photographer she has
worked with most of the
leading advertising
agencies and for *Sunday*
Times Magazine,
Observer Magazine and
Good Housekeeping,
specialising in food
themes, interiors and
portraits. Her work for
cookery books and on
magazine commissions
has taken her in recent
years to India, the United
States, France and Italy.

Hanscomb shoots on a
Wista Field Camera 5 × 4.
Lens: 150mm.
Light: 2 Bowens quad
packs, 1 umbrella and
portable circular reflectors
and tripod.
Filters: CC10Y and
CC05RED.
Film: Ektachrome 100ASA
daylight 5 × 4.

pages:
212-213.

JOHN CLARIDGE

Born in London in 1944,
he had his first individual
exhibition at the age of 17
and has since had 14
more, as well as
participating in group
shows which have been
seen in Britain,
continental Europe, Japan
and the United States.
He has received
over 100 awards for
editorial and commercial
photography, among
them Cleo awards
presented in New York,
Communications Arts
awards given in California,
and D&AD and *Campaign*
press awards in London.

Claridge uses a Deardroff
special Field Camera 5×4
Lens: 65, 75 and 90mm
Light: Available light and
tripod, Polaroids to
determine exposure
Film: 50 ASA
transparency rated
Normal, sometimes
breathes on lens for
atmosphere but
conditions were so wet on
the shoot that the lenses
were pretty diffuse
anyway.

pages:
74-75. 85. 104-105.
106-107. 118-119.

DAVID HURN

A member of the Magnum
Photos co-operative
agency since 1967, he
has had individual
exhibitions in England,
Wales, France, Germany,
United States, Sweden,
Japan, Belgium and
Netherlands and is widely
represented in museum
collections. He was born
in England in 1934 and
has worked as a
photographer since 1955.
His work has been
collected in a book, *David*
Hurn: Photographs
1956-76 (1979). Based in
Wales since 1971, he has
been Head of the School
of Documentary
Photography and Film at
Gwent College of Higher
Education in South Wales,
since 1973.

Hurn uses the Olympus
OM4 system.
Lens: 24mm, 35mm and
50mm.
Light: Flash, Olympus
310, dedicated, 'bounces
off whatever is around',
hand held.
Filters: Cokin sometimes.
Film: Kodachrome 64.

pages:
39. 90-91. 214-215.

GUGLIELMO GALVIN

Born in Dublin in 1939 of
an Italian mother and an
Irish father, he left Ireland
at the age of 16 in a
period of mass
emigration. He worked at
a series of jobs in
London, becoming a
photographer, as he puts
it, "by stealth". He worked
as a photographic printer
and while also involved in
street theatre established
himself as a freelance
photographer in the late
1970s. His principal
outlets have been the
colour magazines of the
Sunday Times and *The*
Observer.

Galvin shoots on
Hasselblad, in colour.
Lens: 40mm and 50mm
Carl Zeiss Distagon.
Light: Norman portable
flash, Polaroids to
determine exposure,
always on tripod.
Film: Ektachrome 64-100
ASA daylight.

pages:
132. 216-217

TOM KELLY

A freelance photographer
since 1975, when he
completed a three-year
course in graphic design
in a London college in a
single year, he was born
in Limerick in 1952 and
worked as a building
labourer in London to
finance his studies. In
1978, after having his first
solo show in London, he
returned to Ireland,
establishing a partnership
with another freelance
photographer with whom
he travelled to China. An
exhibition of their work
there was shown in
Ireland in 1980. A further
exhibition of his work
toured the United States.
He has had commissions
for UNICEF and WHO
calendars involving travel
throughout the world and
has done photography for
many calendars produced
by major Irish commercial
organisations.

Kelly uses a Nikon F2A
and a Mamiya 6 × 4.5.
Lens: Nikon 500mm to
28mm. For the Mamiya
50mm and 80mm.
Light: Available light,
tripod.
Film: Kodachrome 64D
and Ektachrome 100.
Filters: ND's.

pages:
64. 73. 97. 108-109. 110-111.
116-117. 121. 128. 163. 194.
225.

JERRY GORDON

A partner in the New
York-based Wayfarer
photographic agency
which counts *Fortune,*
Ambassador Magazine
and *Philadelphia Magazine*
among its clients. Born in
Chicago in 1949 he
became a professional
photographer after studies
in St. Louis and Chicago.
He has worked as an
advertising and fashion
photographer, a stills
photographer on films,
has had work published in
American, French and
Italian journals and in a
book of his photographs,
Swimmers (1982). Solo
exhibitions have been
presented in a dozen
galleries throughout the
United States and he has
participated in many more
group shows.

Gordon uses the Nikon F3
system.
Lens: 28mm and 35mm.
Light: Vivitar 283, direct
not bounced, long shutter
speeds, ⅛ and ¼ but
hand-held.
Film: Kodachrome 64.

pages:
218-219. 220-221. 269.

BILL KIRK

Born in County Down,
Northern Ireland, in 1937,
he worked as a
draughtsman in the
aircraft industry and as an
audio-visual technician in
a Belfast college before
becoming a full-time
photographer in the
1970s. Following the
publication of his first
book of photographs,
Klondyke Bar (1975), he
was given a 2,000 dollar
award by the Irish
American Cultural
Institute. He has worked
with the Northern Ireland
Tourist Board since 1978,
during which time he has
exhibited in several group
shows and published
Images of Belfast (1983).
Up to his participation in
The Ireland Project, his
work had been confined to
Northern Ireland.

Kirk uses the Olympus
OM2 SP system.
Lens: 60-120 zoom,
28-48 zoom.
Light: Available, wherever
possible.
Film: Ektachrome 100.

pages:
114-115.

EDDIE KULIGOWSKI

He started his career in
photography in 1967, be-
coming an assistant to an
advertising photographer
in 1970, and setting up as
a freelance in 1973, based
in Paris. In 1976, he was
the recipient of the Prix
Niepce. Individual
exhibitions have toured
the United States and
France on several
occasions and he has
taken part in group shows
presented in West
Germany, Netherlands,
Yugoslavia, Belgium, as
well as throughout
France. His work has
been represented in
Italian, American,
Swedish, Dutch, Spanish
and French publications,
in posters, and postcards
and is contained in
permanent collections in
the United States and in
France. He was born in
France in 1946 to parents
of Polish origin.

Kuligowski uses a Contax
RT5.
Lens: 28mm and 35mm.
Light: hand held, available
light.
Film: TRI-X 400 ASA
downrated to 200 ASA
processed in Perceptol.

pages:
86-87. 102-103.

281

Photographers

PETER LAVERY   LONDON, ENGLAND

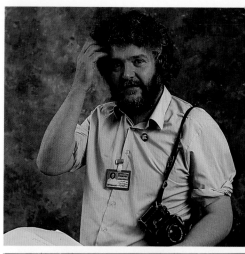

BUZZ LOGAN   BELFAST, IRELAND

MARKETA LUSKACOVA   PRAGUE, CZECHOSLOVAKIA

ALEN MACWEENEY   NEW YORK, USA

PETER MARTENS   ROTTERDAM, NETHERLANDS

VINCENT MENTZEL   ROTTERDAM, NETHERLANDS

FRANK MILLER   DUBLIN, IRELAND

JEREMY NICHOLL   BELFAST, IRELAND

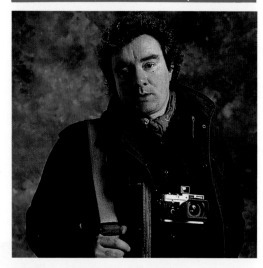

TONY O'SHEA   DUBLIN, IRELAND

BILL OWENS   CALIFORNIA, USA

SUE PACKER   GWENT, WALES

rn in Yorkshire, gland, in 1948, he came a professional otographer following udies at the Royal llege of Art in London. s work has appeared in ropean and American blications.

also works for vertising agencies and s been documenting the e of circuses throughout rope.

very uses a Gandolfi hole plate camera with a × 4 reduction back. so a Victorian "soft cus" portrait camera. ns: 90 and 120mm hneider Copals. ght: Available and xed. Location lights: ofilight, shoulder cks. Indoors: inchron. Tripod. termines exposure &W Polaroids. ters: Grad filters d polariser. m: 5 × 4 Ektachrome 17 and Vericolor Type and L.

ages:
-21. 98-99. 113. 153. 156-7. 173. 206-207. 254-5.

Born in County Antrim, Northern Ireland, in 1943, he worked as a deep-sea fisherman before moving to Dublin in 1968 and starting a career as a photographer. He was a freelance press photographer, then staff photographer with Independent Newspapers group up to 1978 when he moved to Belfast to set up a community photographic project and publishing co-operative in the Shankill Road area of the city. His own book of photographs, *Shankill*, was published in 1979 and in 1982 he established the fortnightly *Shankill Bulletin* of which he is co-director and photographer.

Logan uses the Canon Fl system.
Lens: 50mm.
Light: available light 90% of the time, hand held.
Film: 400ASA, up-rated to 800ASA, processed in D76.

pages:
195. 209.

Born in Prague, Czechoslovakia, in 1944, she studied social sciences, writing a thesis on traditional forms of religious faith in Slovakia, before taking up photography. Her work took her to Ireland in 1972, 1973 and 1974. An exhibition, *Pilgrim*, mounted by the Victoria and Albert Museum, London, started an 18 months tour in 1985. Her work has been published in Swiss, German, Japanese, French and British publications and is widely represented in permanent collections.

Luskacova uses a Leica M4 with 35 and 50mm lenses, also a Canon Fl with 24mm and 50mm lenses
Light: Hand held, available and sometimes Canon autoflash
Film: 400 ASA uprated to 800 ASA

pages:
31. 178-179. 247. 258-259. 261. 273.

Born in Dublin, he started work at the age of 16, as a photographer with *The Irish Times*. He has been based in the United States since 1961 and has worked for many major advertisers and commercial clients as well as contributing to publications such as *Connoisseur, Life, Geo, Fortune, Rolling Stone* and *Esquire*. His work is represented in over 60 permanent collections and has been exhibited in 15 individual and group shows. His commissions have taken him all over the world but he returns frequently to Ireland where he has spent long periods living and working with travelling people.

MacWeeney uses a Nikon F2A with MD2 motordrive.
Lens: 200mm–24mm.
Light: hand held and tripod, available light.
Film: Kodachrome 25D and Ektachrome 400.

pages:
96. 248-249. 270-271.

Born in 1937, he was Dutch Photographer of the Year in 1984. He works for Dutch magazines and for the New York-based agency, Black Star. He has had his work published by a wide range of national and international magazines and newspapers as well as in three books of his photographs, *1/250th at f8* (1979), *Nothing Special* (1983), *Cruel Compassion* (1986). Individual exhibitions have been presented in Holland and abroad and he participated in both the London project (1983) and Los Angeles project (1984).

Martens uses the oldest Nikon system, the Nikon F and Leica CL.
Lens: Nikon 24, 35 and 50mm and 105mm and Leica – 40mm.
Light: hand held available light at all times.
Film: 400ASA uprated to 800ASA.

pages:
242-243. 250-251. 262-263. 274-275.

New York-born, and a graduate of Dartmouth College, New Hampshire, he has been a photographer for ten years and is currently represented by the Daniel Wolf Gallery in New York. Since 1976, when he had his first individual show and participated in his first group exhibition, he has had his work selected for permanent collections in the Museum of Modern Art, New York, San Francisco's Museum of Modern Art, the Houston Museum of Fine Art and the Dallas Art Museum. He had fellowships from the Guggenheim Memorial Foundation in 1978 and 1982. His work has been published in *New Yorker, Modern Photography* and *Art Forum*.

Sternfeld uses a Wista 8×10
Lens: Schneider Symmar S. 360mm
Light: Natural light plus tripod
Film: Vericolour type L and S 8×10

pages:
18-19. 50-51.

staff photographer with e Dutch daily newspaper RC Handelsblad since 973, he has also ntributed to *Newsweek, ime* and the *Sunday imes,* has exhibited equently, mainly in otterdam, and has ublished seven books. hese include *China* 1978), *Foto Vincent Mentzel* (1984) and *Pope Holland* (1985). Born in 945, he studied at the otterdam Academy of ne Arts, has won many wards for his hotography, including laster of Press hotography (1983) and a board member of the /orld Press Photo oundation, based in msterdam.

Mentzel uses the Nikon M & FE systems. ens: 24, 35, 50 and 05mm. ight: hand held, available ght most times. lm: 400ASA uprated to 00ASA and Ektachrome 00ASA.

ages:
8. 181.

Born in Dublin in 1956 he has been a member of the staff of *The Irish Press* since he left school. He worked for five years as an assistant in the dark room, while also studying photography at a Dublin college. Since he became a staff photographer he has three times won Press Photographer of the Year awards in the features section and in the People and News sections. In 1984, he won the Outstanding Feature Picture award in the Benson & Hedges press awards.

Miller works on a Nikon F
Lens: 85mm lens
Light: available light with a tripod
Film: Ektachrome 200 uprated to 400

pages:
52-53.

Born in Belfast in 1957, he studied Art and Design at Jordanstown Polytechnic before moving to London. A full time photographer specialising in news and current affairs since 1981, he works mainly for the British national press including the *Sunday Times* and the *Guardian* and the US magazines, *Time* and *Newsweek*.

Nicholl uses the Canon Fl and Leica M4P
Lens: Canon 24 and 35mm, Leica – 40mm.
Light: Vivitar 283 flash, bounced and direct, no tripod, hand held.
Filters: 81A on Kodachrome.
Film: Kodachrome 64 and 400ASA rated normal.

pages:
44-45. 145.

A freelance photographer since 1980, he spent several years working on building sites in Britain and Ireland and three years travelling in Asia, including teaching English in Japan for a year. His photography has been done mainly for *In Dublin* magazine, also for a group of Swedish magazines. His work was also included in two group exhibitions, *Six Irish Photographers* (1984) and *Out of the Shadows* (1981). Born in Valentia Island, County Kerry, in 1947, he has made Dublin themes his speciality.

O'Shea uses the Leica M2 and M42.
Lens: 28 and 35mm.
Light: hand held, available light most times.
Film: 400ASA uprated to 800ASA, processed in microphen.

pages:
150-151. 154-155. 160-161. 166-167. 190-191.

Now principally a brewer – as owner of Buffalo Bill's Brewery in Hayward, California – his photographic work has been exhibited in solo shows in the United States, Spain, Finland and England and in numerous group shows. Born in California in 1938, he worked as a news photographer 1968-78, publishing a number of books during that period, among them *Suburbia* (1972) and *Documentary Photography: A Personal View* (1978). He received a National Endowment for the Arts Grants in 1974-75, 1977, 1978 and 1979 and a Guggenheim Fellowship in 1976.

Owens borrowed his equipment and wasn't sure which equipment or which flash it was but he thinks it was a Nikon FE. It was definitely lightweight.
Lens: 70–200mm zoom
Light: He thinks it was a Nikon speedlight hand held, also carries a Polaroid snapper to satisfy demanding children
Film: High speed Ektachrome 200

pages:
182. 237.

A freelance portrait photographer since 1981, following studies in art and photography in Wales and England and winning *The Observer* photography prize in 1979. Her work has been exhibited in a number of shows at the Ffoto Gallery in Cardiff, South Wales, also in *Contemporary European Portraiture* (1983) shown in Arizona, USA, in *Women European Photographers Today* (1985), shown in Amsterdam, Netherlands, and in *Portrait Photography by British Photographers*, 1935-85, shown in Impressions Gallery, York, England. She participated in *A Day in the Life of London* (1983). Born in Wales in 1954, she has been a part-time lecturer at Gwent College of Higher Education since 1983.

Packer uses the Bronica SQ system.
Lens: 80mm.
Light: 2 Workhorse 500 J's with two umbrellas (battery packs) with tripod, mixing with available light.
Film: B&W 125ASA, rated normal.

pages:
171. 256-257.

Photographers

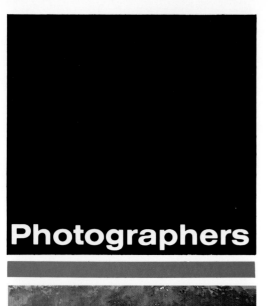

MARTIN PARR   CHESHIRE, ENGLAND

BARRIE ROKEACH   CALIFORNIA, USA

RED SAUNDERS   LONDON, ENGLAND

SYD SHELTON   LONDON, ENGLAND

BILLY STICKLAND   DUBLIN, IRELAND

GERAY SWEENEY   COUNTY TYRONE, IRELAND

PIERRE TOUTAIN   PARIS, FRANCE

CHARLES TRAUB   NEW YORK, USA

RENATE VON FORSTER   FRANKFURT, GERMANY

JAKE WALLIS   LONDON, ENGLAND

DENIS WAUGH   DUNEDIN NEW ZEALAND

MARTIN PARR

Following studies in photography at Manchester Polytechnic, 1970-73, he worked as a photojournalist and lecturer in both Britain and Ireland, as well as contributing to magazines and working on commissions for exhibitions. His work has been seen in solo shows in England, Spain, the Netherlands, Ireland, Sweden and the United States, also in many group exhibitions. His book of photographs of the West of Ireland, *A Fair Day*, was published in 1984. His other books are *Bad Weather* (1982) and *Prescot Now and Then* (1984).

Parr uses the Plaubell Makina 6 × 7 system. Lens: Fixed lenses, 55mm and 80mm. Light: mixed, available and flash, Vivitar 283 with reflector always shoots horizontal not vertical. Film: Vericolour negative 100ASA.

pages: 22-23. 24-25. 36-37. 60-61. 76-77. 172. 186-187. 222-223. 228-229.

BARRIE ROKEACH

A professional photographer for 15 years, he has taught at the University of California, in Berkeley, has exhibited in Los Angeles, San Francisco, New York and Chicago, and worked on commissions for corporate clients such as Chevron, Kodak and Sierra Club. His work has been published in *Scientific American, Fortune, Time, Life,* and many more leading magazines and journals. He has been a pilot for 19 years and specialises in aerial photography, piloting himself while he also takes photographs.

Rokeach uses the Nikon F3 system. Lens: 105, 135, 200 and 300mm. No clamps or tripods, hand held, shutter wide open with very fast lenses. Film: Kodachrome 64.

pages: 13. 32-33. 49. 68-69. 92-93. 109. 232-233.

RED SAUNDERS

Born in London in 1945, photographer since 1963. Has worked on photographic commissions for many of the leading international magazines, including *Fortune, Esquire,* and *Rolling Stone* in the United States and *Sunday Times* magazine in Britain. He contributed to *A Day In The Life of New Zealand* (1983) and his assignments have also taken him to Europe, the Caribbean, United States and the South Pacific.

Saunders works on Hasselblad ELM. Lens: 40 & 120mm, Carl Zeiss Distagon. Light: Norman portable flash, Polaroids to determine exposure. Generally on tripod, mostly mixing flash with available light. Film: Ektachrome 100ASA daylight.

pages: 72. 130-131. 133. 158-159.

SYD SHELTON

A freelance designer and photographer since 1968, working in London and Sydney, Australia, he was joint organiser of the London project (1983) and shared creative responsibilities for the Los Angeles project (1984) with Red Saunders. As a graphic designer, he has worked on magazines, journals, record sleeves, book covers and posters. He was responsible for the art direction of the London and Los Angeles books as well as being a contributing photographer and a founder of Photo Projects Ltd. He was born in Yorkshire in 1947.

Shelton uses the Nikon F3 system. Lens: 24mm and 500mm. Light: Metz flash, hand held, fill in mix. Film: Kodachrome 64.

pages: 66-67. 204-205.

BILLY STICKLAND

He worked in advertising photography after completing studies at Trinity College, Dublin. He has been a freelance sports photographer since 1981, winning national awards for his work in rugby and Gaelic games in 1984. His photographs have appeared principally in the *Sunday Tribune* and *Magill* magazine but have also been published internationally by *Sports Illustrated* and *Allsport*. He was born in Dublin in 1955.

Stickland works on a Nikon F3T and F2A Lens: 400mm 3.5 Light: available light, hand held and monopod Film: Ektachrome 100 ASA

page: 237.

DEREK SPEIRS

Born in Dublin in 1952, he worked in a photo finishing laboratory in County Dublin after leaving school and began his professional career as a photographer in London, working with the Report co-operative of photographers. In 1978, he returned to Dublin to establish an agency and a library along similar lines, also operating under the name, Report. He specialises in coverage of politics, current affairs and the activities of the labour movement. His photographs are published regularly in a wide range of national and international magazine and newspapers and have been included in many exhibitions on topical social issues.

Speirs uses the Canon new F1 system Lens: 135mm Light: hand held, available light Film: 400 ASA processed straight

pages: 126-127. 168-169.

FERAY SWEENEY

A freelance photographer based in Belfast in 1977-81, she moved to London in 1981 and worked for two years as a photographic assistant before becoming a full-time photographer. Her work since then has included portraits and editorial photography, as well as record sleeves and commissions for film and television companies. She has also participated in Arts Council-sponsored exhibitions. Born in Northern Ireland in 1953, she studied at art colleges in Derby and Guildford, in England.

Sweeney uses Olympus OM2 and Hasselblad. Lens: Olympus 24 and 50mm – Hass – 50, 80 & 150mm. Light: Sunpak flash, hand held and tripod. Filters: on page 267 – 81EF soft are ND over sky and 80 blue grad. Film: Kodachrome 64, Ektachrome 100ASA and Ektachrome Tungsten 64 ASA.

pages: 70-71. 184-185. 252-253. 267.

PIERRE TOUTAIN

Toutain, a native of Normandy, has travelled all over the globe on assignments for such publications as *Stern, Paris Match, Time,* and *Le Figaro*. Photos from tours of Vietnam and Kampuchea were included in a striking exhibition of "Children in The War". He participated in the London and Los Angeles projects.

Toutain uses the Canon FI system. Lens: 105 micro. Light: hand held, available. Film: Kodachrome 64.

page: 266.

CHARLES TRAUB

He has had a dozen solo shows of his photography over the past ten years, from an exhibition of pictures of the Cajun people of Louisiana (1975) to *Nudes* (1984). He has taught at a number of colleges, founded the Chicago Center for Contemporary Photography, was for two years a director of the Light Gallery, New York, and has been a consulting editor for several publishing houses. In 1982, he was commissioned by the city of Naples, Italy, to document the life of the city. His photographs of beach scenes were published in a book, *Beach* (1981). He is a partner in Wayfarer Photographic Agency, working for some of the United States' leading publications.

Traub uses the Nikon F3 system. Lens: 25-55 zoom. Light: available and mixed – Vivitar 283 flash with a Quantum battery pack – hand held. Film: Kodachrome 64 and high speed Ektachrome.

pages: 40-41. 42-43. 140-141. 142-143. 146-147. 174-175. 177.

RENATE VON FORSTER

One of the 17 members of the Bilderberg photographic agency and archive, based in Hamburg, she has been a full-time freelance photographer since 1973. She was born in Nüremberg in May 1948 and studied photography at college in Hofheim, Hessen. Her first professional work was in the television and film business. In the late 1970s, she became a regular contributor to *Die Zeit* magazine and has, since 1979, worked on assignments for a number of international publications, including *Stern, Geo, New York Times Magazine,* and *Sunday Times Magazine*. She has had three books published.

Von Forster uses the Nikon FA2 system. Lens: 24, 35, 50, 105 and 200mm. Light: mixed – National PE flash, direct and bounced. Film: Kodachrome 64 and Ektachrome 400ASA high speed.

pages: 65. 183. 202-203. 226-227. 264-265.

JAKE WALLIS

An art student for a single year in his native Sussex, England, he worked as a lumberjack in Sweden and travelled widely in continental Europe before becoming a photographer's assistant to Angus McBean. His first job was to print 40,000 contacts and he won an Ilford-sponsored printing competition. In 1970, when MacBean retired, he gave Wallis his studio. Since then, he was worked freelance, doing some advertising work, notably for clients Saab and Renault. He had an individual exhibition of his work at the Olympus Gallery, London, in 1983.

Wallis uses the Synar Norma Monorail system Lens: Schneider Symmar 65 and 90mm Light: available light on tripod, b&w polaroid to determine exposure Filters: 81EF inside camera, neutral grad and colour filters outside plastic bin liners over camera to protect from the elements Film: Ektachrome 6117 200ASA pushed 1 stop

pages: 56-57. 82-83. 88-89. 94-95. 100-101. 231.

DENIS WAUGH

Born in Dunedin, New Zealand, in 1941, he has been based in London for 19 years, having been one of the first two students of stills photography at the Royal College of Art, London. Before these studies, he had worked as an art director in an advertising agency. As a professional photographer he worked first for trade journals, record companies and, since 1978, for the *Sunday Times Magazine*. He has been commissioned by most of the leading British magazines and his work has also appeared in leading US publications such as *Fortune, Esquire, Life, Geo* and *New York Times*.

Waugh uses a Deardorff whole plate camera with a 5 × 4 reduction back. Lens: 75 and 90mm Schneider Symmars. Light: available and mixed. Indoors: Elinchron direct heads diffusers. Tripod. B&W 55PN Polaroid to determine exposure. Film: 5 × 4 Ektachrome 6117 and 6122. Filters: 6-7 filters "depending which way the wind blows".

pages: 34-35. 46-47.

Production Team

KIM ARMITAGE	**ADMINISTRATOR**
ANTHONY CRONIN	**WRITER**
JOHN ELLIS	**MANAGING EDITOR**
JERRY FITZPATRICK	**RESEARCH EDITOR**
BILL HAYES	**RESEARCHER**
JULIEN J.	**PRODUCTION ASSISTANT**
GRAINNE MORBY	**RESEARCH EDITOR**
JENNIFER O'NEILL	**RESEARCHER**
RED SAUNDERS	**EDITOR**
SYD SHELTON	**EDITOR**
BRIAN TRENCH	**CONSULTANT EDITOR**

KIM ARMITAGE

After three years' work with the theatre company, Belt and Braces, she joined The Ireland Project. Previously, she studied psychology at the City of London Polytechnic and travelled and worked in North America. In 1985, she took up a post in the press and publicity department of the National Film Theatre, London.

JULIEN J.

Born in London in 1958, he lived for some years in the West Indies, from where his family came, before returning to England. First became interested in photography while on a youth training scheme for the unemployed at the age of 17, but later worked as a sales assistant and watch repairer before becoming an assistant in a photographic studio. He has had photographs published in West Indian papers and magazines and specialises in photography of musicians, often travelling on the road with rock and reggae bands.

uses the Nikon FE system.
Lens: 24mm.
Light: Nikon speedlight flash, plus tripod.
Film: Kodachrome 64.

age:
3.

JUDE BOWLES

An arts administrator and publicist since 1980, she was born in Shropshire, England, in 1955 and studied at the New University of Ulster in Northern Ireland. She has worked with Ireland's leading theatre companies, the Abbey Theatre and Field Day, as well as with festival and exhibition organisers. In 1985, she was administrator of a national training programme for community arts organisers.

GRAINNE MORBY

She has been working since 1978 as a research and information officer with a London-based resource centre for community advice services throughout Britain. Following studies at Essex University, England, she had worked as an information officer with the National Association of Citizens' Advice Bureaux. She was born in Wakefield, Yorkshire in 1951.

ANTHONY CRONIN

Poet, novelist, critic and essayist, he contributes a column to *The Irish Times* on cultural and political affairs. A selection of these articles has been published in book form, *An Irish Eye* (1958). For three years he was cultural adviser to the Taoiseach (Irish prime minister) and played a central role in the establishment of the artists' assembly, Aosdana, and the accompanying grants system. Among his published works are two comic novels, *Life of Riley* (1964) and *Identity Papers* (1975) a memoir of the exploits of Irish writers in the 1950s, *Dead as Doornails* (1973), and a book of literary criticism, *Heritage Now* (1983). His published poems includes *41 Sonnet Poems 82* (1982) and *Letter to an Englishman* (1985).

JENNIFER O'NEILL

Born in 1952, O'Neill was educated at Roslyn Park in Dublin and Freiburg university in West Germany. She has worked in Germany, Switzerland and Spain and speaks fluent French and German. Returning home to Dublin, she enrolled at the Dublin Institute of Technology to study photography and graduated with distinction in 1985. She was assistant to a professional photographer before opening up her own studio in 1985 specialising in portraiture. She is married with a daughter.

JOHN ELLIS

Born in Bristol in 1948 he is a chartered accountant, who trained with a leading City of London firm, and has worked since 1977 in the entertainment industry, as a producer and manager of theatre and television productions, concerts and festivals and administrator of theatre companies. He was the producer of a production of *Accidental Death of an Anarchist,* by Dario Fo, which transferred from a fringe theatre to London's West End, to run there for 20 months and later to be reproduced as a television play. He is a founder of Photo Projects Ltd who joined the Los Angeles project (1984) as a production consultant and oversaw the management of the Ireland project.

RED SAUNDERS

A founder of Photo Projects Ltd, and joint organiser of the London and Los Angeles Projects. As well as a photographer he has also continued his activities as an actor, an organiser of musical festivals, theatre production and other cultural events, while directing and producing the three major photo book events; *A day in the Life of London, 24 hours in the Life of Los Angeles* and *The Ireland Project.*

JERRY FITZPATRICK

Born in Sheffield in 1949 of Irish parents, he did trade union studies at the Middlesex Polytechnic and has worked as an organiser of the actors' trade union, Equity, and of cultural events in London and Belfast, notably with Rock Against Racism. Since 1982, he has worked with a community advice service sponsored by the Greater London Council.

SYD SHELTON

A freelance designer and photographer in London and Sydney, Australia, Syd Shelton was joint conceptualiser-organiser on the London project and shared the creative responsibilties of the Los Angeles project with Red Saunders; he was primarily responsible for the art direction, design layout of both books and was also a contributing photographer.

BILL HAYES

Born in London in 1949 of a Waterford family. He attended Sir William Grimshaw School in Muswell Hill, London, and North East London Polytechnic. He has worked as a journalist on various trade publications, music press, and Braden's Week (BBC TV), before starting a community newspaper in North London.
In 1981 his book, 'History of World Railways' was published, and for the past five years has been a freelance production organiser for advertising and Editorial photography. He worked in this capacity on the London and LA projects. He now lives in Shoreditch with his 14 year old son. With strong family links with the country he feels that Ireland is probably the most civilised country in Europe.

BRIAN TRENCH

Dublin-based journalist, appointed Managing Editor, *Sunday Tribune,* in 1985, having previously been News Editor with that newspaper. He started in journalism as a freelance in London in 1970, returning to Ireland in 1972, and joining *Hibernia* magazine in 1973. From 1978 to 1981 he was a freelance reporter, first in Dublin, then in Portugal and Spain. Born in Drogheda, Ireland, in 1945, he has also been a critic of jazz and popular music for ten years and has contributed to numerous journals, magazines, radio and television programmes on music and current affairs.

ACKNOWLEDGEMENTS

Monika Baker

Rund Bom

John Bourke

Matthew Boyd, Shamrock Cottages

Brendan Tours

Kevin Brodbin

Peter Butler

Patricia Campion

Gerry Corr, Department of Foreign Affairs, Dublin

Dave Craig

Andy Dark

Drumlease Glebe House, Dromahair

The Dunnes and all at Hassett & Fitzsimons

Mary Finan, Wilson Hartnell Public Relations

Isabella Forbes

John Furlong

Great Southern Hotels

Margaret Greene

Ruth Gregory

Derek Hand

James Higgins

John Hoey

Susan Holland

Enda Hopkins, Iona National Airways

Kate Horgan

Gillian Humble

Irish Distillers

Island House, Sherkin Island

Keith Johnson Photographic

Jim Kirby, Aer Lingus, London

Linda Jane Lancaster

Pete Locker

Colin Mahony

Gerry Malone, Bord Fáilte

Billy McCannon

John McKeever, Orbact Computers, Dublin

Sean McKernan

Miniphoto Limited, Dublin

Teresa Mooney

Jim Moore

National Dairy Council

Liam Neary

Bryan O'Brien

Criona O'Flaherty

Seán O'Riordáin, Park Public Relations

Nigel Posf, Orbact Computers, Dublin

Roger Protz

Danny Rourke

All at The Stag

Nina Saunders

Shannon Free Airport Development Co Ltd

Terry Trench

Jerry Walsh, Raftery Rooms, Kiltimagh

The Wests of Dún Laoghaire